A DOUBTER'S GUIDE
TO THE BIBLE

A DOUBTER'S GUIDE TO THE BIBLE

INSIDE HISTORY'S BESTSELLER
FOR BELIEVERS AND SKEPTICS

JOHN DICKSON

ZONDERVAN

A Doubter's Guide to the Bible
Copyright © 2014 by John Dickson

This title is also available as a Zondervan ebook.
Visit www.zondervan.com/ebooks.

Requests for information should be addressed to:

Zondervan, 3900 *Sparks Dr. SE, Grand Rapids, Michigan 49546*

Library of Congress Cataloging-in-Publication Data

Dickson, John P., 1967-
    A doubter's guide to the Bible : inside history's bestseller for
  believers and skeptics / John Dickson.
      pages cm
    ISBN 978-0-310-51843-3 (softcover)
    1. Bible — Introductions. I. Title.
  BS475.3.D53 2015
  220.6'1 — dc23   2014021663

Cover design: Studio Gearbox
Interior design: David Conn

Printed in the United States of America

HB 01.26.2022

For Elsie Faithorn
who taught me "The Lord's Prayer"
before I knew anything about
the Lord or prayer

Thanks to

- Casey Ankers for transcribing the rambling lectures that got this book going
- Kate Wilcox for editorial and research assistance
- Claire Fern for fresh eyes on the Bible
- J. R. for masterful "library support"
- Jenny Glen for ten wonderful years working as my assistant

CONTENTS

A PUBLISHER'S DREAM

The Bible is history's number one bestseller by a factor of about ten. Six billion copies have been sold. Admittedly, it had a head start on other books; it was the first item off the modern printing press. But it has been Number One every year since records have been kept—except for 2007, when *Harry Potter and the Deathly Hallows* topped the list, with forty-four million sales. Unlike most bestsellers, however, the Bible actually *increases* sales each year. Harry Potter's forty-four million in a year is spectacular, but no doubt it dropped to about ten million the following year, one million the next, and now *Deathly Hallows* probably sells in the mere hundreds of thousands.

The latest figures for the Bible are hard to fathom. It sold thirty million copies in 2009 alone. That is 82,000 copies a day, 3,400 copies an hour. That means someone gets a Bible every second—perhaps sixty copies have changed hands since you started reading this page. If we were to include the sales of individual portions of the Bible, such as books containing just the Gospels (the four biographies of Jesus), you have to multiply these numbers by a factor of twelve. The Bible is available in 2,500 languages, Harry Potter in just fifty-five.

WHY IS THE BIBLE SO POPULAR?

One answer to this question about the Bible's popularity is linked to the church's *power*. Some people think of a domineering Vatican or some dark right-wing lobby imposing the Bible wherever it goes. I think that gets things the wrong way around. The church does not create the Bible; the Bible creates the church. Proof of this in the modern world is the situation in China. No one argues the Bible is being imposed on the Chinese, who have been under atheistic communist rule for decades. However, just recently, Amity Press in Nanjing had a public celebration for the 100 millionth Bible published in China. Today this monumental printing company, which I recently had the pleasure of visiting, produces twelve million Bibles a year, making up one third of all Bibles published in the world. Such figures make it difficult to sustain the argument that the church is imposing its holy book. The Bible has its own life, its own uncanny attraction.

I believe the Bible is so popular and influential because it tells a story we recognize as true. I don't just mean it tells an accurate story—though it is telling that the Bible stands tall even after more than two hundred years of secular criticism. What I mean is that its account of humanity and the world we live in *rings true*. Reading the Bible can be like meeting someone you don't know who, oddly, somehow seems to know *you* deeply. It is uncanny. Sometimes when you read the Bible, you find yourself asking, "How does this book know that about me? How does it know that about our world—especially when it was written so long ago?"

When you read the Bible, it is as though it *reads you*. And it is my hope that as you dip your toe into the Bible's story and viewpoint, you will find yourself feeling that the Good Book knows more about the world—and about you—than any normal book does.

MY GOAL

This little book is an ambitious attempt to unpack the whole Bible or, perhaps more accurately, to give a sense of the whole biblical narrative and of the "theology" that emerges from it. More than that, I want to offer a snapshot of the worldview and lifestyle the Bible inspires.

This is probably more than anyone should attempt in so slim a book. The Bible itself, in most editions, runs to about a thousand pages. The walls of my office are lined with hundreds of commentaries on the biblical texts, literally hundreds of thousands of pages devoted to exploring the history and meaning of the Scriptures. As for giving insight into what it means to *live* in the light of the Bible, greater minds and better human beings than I have written about authentic Christian living.

If I can assume these confessions haven't put you off, the value of this book is that it offers something of a "biblical primer" for those who aren't sure what to make of the Bible. Whatever our beliefs, there is still enormous value in getting our heads around why this book, like no other, has shaped the lives of millions of people for thousands of years (with no sign of letting up). This is not really an exercise in "apologetics"—the art of trying to prove the truth of the

Bible—but a simple outline for curious doubters of what it might mean for life if the Bible happened to be true.

A BIBLICAL ROAD MAP

In the chapters that follow I have attempted to recount some of the most important stories, moments, and characters from the Bible. More than this, I have attempted to show the overarching narrative of the Bible, a story that stretches from creation to eternity, giving everything in between a particular shape and substance. In Bible-speak, this is called "salvation history" or "biblical theology," an account of how God planned, revealed, and executed his purposes for the world.

Because the Bible is so big, it can be difficult to get a handle on the significance of a particular story, or even to know how to read it. Simply opening a page at random can feel like sitting down in the middle of an episode of *Downton Abbey*. You spend half the time asking, "Who's that?" "Why are they arguing?" "What does that mean?" "Why do they talk funny!?" It helps to have a basic framework.

The Bible recounts the interaction of God with his people. It is split into two sections, the Old Testament (OT) and the New Testament (NT). The Old Testament is the record of God's dealings with his chosen people, Israel, and covers the time period from the "Beginning"—whenever that was—to roughly 500 BC. The New Testament begins with the birth of Jesus (shortly before the AD 1 mark), tells of his life, teaching, death, and resurrection, and includes numerous texts written to the first generation or two of Christian believers, up to the end of the first century.

Perhaps the key thing to remember about how Christians read this big book is that they have always insisted on two simple things: first, that the Old Testament *points forward* to what Jesus would do in the New Testament; and, second, that we must therefore read the Old Testament *through the lens* of the New Testament. What this means in practice will become clear throughout the book.

Many important books have been written on this theme, but I don't think you can get past the classic by Graeme Goldsworthy, *Gospel and Kingdom: A Christian Interpretation of the Old Testament* (Paternoster, 2012); or Vaughan Roberts, *God's Big Picture: Tracing the Storyline of the Bible* (InterVarsity Press, 2003). Perhaps the best "textbook" on the Bible, written for the general public not just church folk, is still *The Lion Handbook to the Bible* (4th ed., Lion Books, 2009; also published as *The Zondervan Handbook to the Bible*), an extraordinary text, complete with hundreds of maps, images, and tables, that walks readers through each section of the Bible explaining both its history and meaning.

BOOK NOTES

You could also break the Bible down according to literary style. Much of the Bible is written as history, as it recounts the events of the Israelite nation. This is true of books like Exodus, Joshua, Kings, Chronicles, and others. The New Testament also contains lots of history, as it

ISRAEL'S HISTORY ROUGHLY FOLLOWS THIS TRAJECTORY:

— Creation (key players: Adam and Eve)
— The fall (Adam and Eve)
— God makes promises to Abraham
— Israel in slavery in Egypt (Joseph and brothers)
— God rescues Israel from Egypt (Moses)
— Israel enters the Promised Land (Joshua)
— Israel ruled by judges (Gideon, Deborah, Samson, etc.)
— Israel gets its first king (King Saul)
— King David becomes king
— Kings rule (mostly badly) for four hundred years
— Prophets warn Israel of God's coming punishment on the nation (while also promising a glorious future beyond judgment)
— Exile, part one: Israel (the northern half), conquered by Assyria
— Exile, part two: Judah (the southern half), conquered by Babylon
— Many Israelites return to Israel to rebuild the demolished land and temple
— Lots of waiting for the "new covenant," which the prophets promised
— This is where the New Testament picks up the story of Jesus

recounts the life of Jesus in the Gospels and the story of the early church in the book of Acts.

Some books of the Old Testament are full of laws that the Israelite people were to uphold. These books, which include Leviticus, Numbers, and Deuteronomy, do not generally make for page-turning reading, but they are an important part of understanding God's relationship with his people. The

New Testament epistles or letters also contain "laws," or at least the application of Christian ethics to everyday life.

Some Old Testament books record prophecies: for instance, Isaiah, Jeremiah, Ezekiel, Amos, Micah, and Jonah. Prophets were God's messengers to his people, which he often sent to tell the Israelites when they were sinning, warning them to return to him. Only one New Testament text is filled with prophecy, the book of Revelation, the last portion of the Bible.

Finally, some of the books of the Old Testament have been grouped together into the genre of Wisdom Literature. They include Job, Psalms, Proverbs, Ecclesiastes, Song of Songs, and Lamentations. These books are full of rich reflections on life and God and articulate the human predicament of love, suffering, wisdom, joy, feelings of futility, and feelings of hope. While the present book focuses on the larger narrative of the Bible, along the way I will include brief texts from the Wisdom Literature, as they provide beautiful insight into the richness of the spiritual life. Much of the material in the New Testament letters mentioned above has the character of this Wisdom Literature as the apostles direct the members of their churches to apply Christ's wisdom to a myriad of daily experiences.

1

HOW EVERYTHING IS GOOD:
THE CREATION STORY

GOD SAW ALL THAT HE HAD MADE, AND IT WAS VERY GOOD. AND THERE
WAS EVENING, AND THERE WAS MORNING – THE SIXTH DAY.

(GENESIS 1:31)

The first thing we confront when we open the Bible is the radical claim that the world is *good*. I say "radical" not because Westerners today will think this idea is terribly revolutionary but because when the Bible was written, this was not a widely held view. The biblical idea of the goodness of the world has infused the thinking of most people in Western culture, regardless of their faith perspective; but when the Old Testament first tried out the idea, it was novel.

The first scene of the Bible states it simply:

> In the beginning God created the heavens and the earth. Now the earth was formless and empty, darkness was over the surface of the deep, and the Spirit of God was hovering over the waters.

And God said, "Let there be light," and there was light. God saw that the light was good. (Genesis 1:1 – 4a)

Then follows the story of the rest of the creation, with the deliberate repetition of the words "it was good." Here's an executive summary:

(Genesis 1:10) God called the dry ground "land," and the gathered waters he called "seas." And God saw that it was good.

(Genesis 1:12) The land produced vegetation: plants bearing seed according to their kinds and trees bearing fruit with seed in it according to their kinds. And God saw that it was good.

(Genesis 1:16, 18) God made two great lights ... to govern the day and the night, and to separate light from darkness. And God saw that it was good.

(Genesis 1:21) So God created the great creatures of the sea and every living thing with which the water teems and that moves about in it, according to their kinds, and every winged bird according to its kind. And God saw that it was good.

(Genesis 1:25) God made the wild animals according to their kinds, the livestock according to their kinds, and all the creatures that move along the ground according to their kinds. And God saw that it was good.

(Genesis 1:31) God saw all that he had made, and it was very good.

The opening point of the Bible is striking: a good God created a good world in which he placed good people to do good work. Everything is good.

THE CONTROVERSY OF GENESIS 1

Before I go further, I should say a little about my view of Genesis 1. For some, this part of Holy Scripture, with its emphasis on God creating the world in six days, is a huge obstacle to taking the Bible seriously. For others, it is the test case of whether one takes the Bible seriously. It needn't be either.

I do not believe Genesis 1 was ever meant to be read in a *concrete* way. The literary style in the original Hebrew (still observable in English) is not identical to historical prose, such as you find from Genesis 12 on or in the books of the Kings or in the much later Gospels. Most experts agree with this. Genesis 1 isn't quite poetry, such as we find in the book of Psalms, but neither is it exactly prose. With a striking saturation of literary devices, Genesis 1 sits somewhere between poetry and prose—what you might call an *ode*. It is an "ode to creation" or, perhaps more accurately, an "ode to the Creator."

Old Testament specialist Bill T. Arnold calls it a "creation overture," alluding to the way an opera might open with some of the key themes and tunes to be developed later. "The Bible's first chapter has an elegant prose more akin to poetry and may, in fact, have been based on a poem originally.... Its position at the head of the Bible means it charts the course for the reader" (Bill T. Arnold, *Genesis* [Cambridge University Press, 2008], 29).

Old Testament specialists regularly point out the rhyme, rhythm, repetition, and artistic structure of Genesis 1. These (in the minds of many but certainly not all) indicate that the author is trying to convey his point in a highly literary way. Adding to this impression is the use throughout the opening chapter of the number seven. In Hebrew literary tradition the number seven was the number of perfection, the number of wholeness and of the divine. It was used in all sorts of literature to convey the theme. Indeed, the traditional Jewish menorah or seven-candle lampstand, the symbol of the modern state of Israel, comes from this same ancient biblical motif.

The opening sentence of the Bible contains just seven words in Hebrew (though it obviously differs in translation). The crucial phrase "And it was so" is repeated seven times in this opening ode. The words "and it was good" also appear exactly seven times. And there is the obvious fact that the whole account is structured around seven scenes or seven days. *Multiples* of seven also appear in uncanny ways. The second sentence of the ode contains fourteen words (2 x 7). "God" appears thirty-five times (5 x 7). "Earth" and "heaven/firmament," the two halves of the created order, are each named twenty-one times (3 x 7) (so, Gordon Wenham, *Genesis 1 – 15* [Word, 1987], 6).

This combination of literary devices in Genesis 1 is most unusual and is never found in this concentrated way in historical prose elsewhere in the Bible. Pretty much everyone agrees with that. This observation convinces me, and many others, that the main point of the Bible's creation account is not historical or scientific but literary, theological, and philosophical. It is this deeper point that the original author wants us to focus on. I would go as far as to say that even if scientists next week proved that the world was made in just six days, six thousand years ago, I would still maintain that this is *not* what the author of Genesis was getting at in his opening ode.

Let me offer a comparison. Imagine if historians were able to prove that the famous parable Jesus told about the Good Samaritan — where a Jewish man is beaten and left for dead on the Jericho road, and then is cared for by a Samaritan — also turned out to be a true historical narrative. Even if we found evidence that these events occurred in time and space exactly as Luke 10 recounts, I would still contend that Jesus' retelling of the narrative was a *parable* with a moral or symbolic point and was not an intended historical report. I feel the same about Genesis 1. Many fellow Christians disagree with me, and that is fine; I do not want to be dogmatic about this, and nor do I want to cast my Six-Day Creationist friends as naïve. However, I do want to insist that the central point of Genesis 1 is not the pressing scientific question of modern men and women but the more pressing theological and philosophical questions that have haunted humanity for all history.

In passing, I also want to mention that those who hold a more symbolic view of Genesis 1 are in very good, and very old, company. Long before modern science began to pose difficult questions to the biblical text, numerous ancient theologians, like Clement of Alexandria (third century AD) and Saint Augustine of Hippo (fifth century AD), interpreted the six days of Genesis as a symbol of the orderliness of creation. Indeed, even before these giants of the Christian church, the first-century Jewish intellectual Philo of Alexandria took the "six days" to be a deliberate literary device designed by the author of Genesis to convey the deep structure and organization of the created world (Philo, *De opificio mundi* 13). And the leading Jewish scholar of the Middle

Ages, Moses Maimonides (twelfth century), insisted that the creation story is to be read figuratively, not concretely (Maimonides, *Guide for the Perplexed*, 2.29).

My point here is not that because some clever people in the past held a nonconcrete view of Genesis 1, so should we. I am merely underlining that these revered figures of Jewish and Christian history came to their views about Genesis *centuries before* the rise of evolutionary science and evidence of deep geological time. It is simply wrong to suggest, as some contemporary atheists imagine, that a symbolic reading of this part of the Bible is a watering-down or liberalization of biblical faith inspired by the great torrent of modern science.

I am saddened when my Six-Day Creationist friends—and I am pleased to say I have a few—tell me I am not taking the Bible seriously. I reply that I genuinely believe that the symbolic reading of Genesis 1 is the more sensitive and faithful reading of this foundational scriptural text (and in view of Philo's comments above, we can also describe it as the *oldest* interpretation we know of). The view I am advocating is probably the majority view of mainstream churches today (taking a global, multi-denominational perspective), but Christians have freedom to disagree on this matter. I am also happy for readers to disagree with me, because the key points of the Genesis narrative remain true regardless of what we think of this debate.

It is probably worth pointing out, if only in passing, that there are a few major passages and themes in the Bible where Christians come to different views. Genesis 1 is an obvious fault line, but there are others. I imagine it leaves the outside observer wondering how we know when to take Scripture concretely and when to take a more symbolic view. The best I can say is that where there are genuine, significant disagreements between equally informed and devoted Christians (as opposed to those who are looking to create God in their own image), it is probably a sign that the Author—with a capital A—is granting us some slack. This does not mean that everything is up for grabs or that you can make the Bible say whatever you want. Far more impressive than these disagreements are the plentiful shared convictions of Christians of all stripes down through history. There is a profound basic plotline and vision for life in the Bible. That's where we should form our strongest opinions. That is the focus of this book.

A PAGAN CREATION

What, then, are the main theological points of the Bible's opening chapter (whether or not we also take the "six days" concretely)? In answering this, we must consider the beliefs of the cultures that surrounded the Bible's original audience.

In the nineteenth century archaeologists discovered stone tablets narrating a story that dates from around the same time as Moses, the traditional author of Genesis. It is called *Enuma Elish* ("When on High"), and although its precise origins and date are still a matter of debate, its central claims about creation are almost certainly representative of convictions held throughout the non-Jewish world of the second millennium BC.

Enuma Elish was a Babylonian masterpiece. It is a seven-part story found on seven tablets and was recited every New

Year's Day as a kind of reminder of the order of the universe. It opens in a watery chaos, out of which the gods arise and conduct an enormous celestial war. As a result of combat, the bits and pieces of the wounded gods form the universe: this limb of a defeated god becomes the earth, another the sky, and so on. In the sixth scene on the sixth tablet humankind is made. Interestingly, they are crafted as an afterthought. The vanquished gods cry out to the king god, Marduk, that it is unfair that they should be his slaves for eternity. After all, they are gods! They entreat Marduk to create some other beast that could serve him his daily food. Marduk, being a benevolent dictator, declares:

> When Marduk hears the words of the gods, his heart prompts him to fashion artful works. Opening his mouth, he addresses Ea to impart the plan he had conceived in his heart: "Blood I will mass and cause bones to be. I will establish a savage, Man shall be his name. Truly, savage man I will create. He shall be charged with the service of the gods that they [the gods] might be at ease!" ... They bound Kinju, holding him before Ea. They imposed on him his guilt and severed his blood vessels. Out of his blood they fashioned mankind. He imposed the service and let free the gods. (*Enuma Elish*, Tablet 6, lines 1–8, 31–34. Translation found in Bill T. Arnold and Bryan E. Beyer, *Readings from the Ancient Near East* [Baker, 2002], 42–43)

Genesis 1 has undeniable affinities with *Enuma Elish*. It, too, begins with a watery chaos. It has the same basic order of creation. Human beings are also created in the sixth scene. This may be accidental, indicative simply of a shared cultural environment. And no one (anymore) thinks the Bible is simply copying *Enuma Elish* (the texts come from roughly the same time, but we can't be sure which was composed first). It is likely that the Genesis narrative mirrors pagan forms of thought, whether in *Enuma Elish* or elsewhere, in an effort to overthrow them.

GENESIS VERSUS PAGANISM

There are similarities between Genesis 1 and *Enuma Elish*, but the contrasts are far more striking. Ancient people aware of pagan ideas would have spotted several subversive ideas in Genesis 1. *Enuma Elish* opens with nine gods in the first paragraphs, but Genesis enjoys telling us, "In the beginning God created the heavens and the earth." Instantly, we are transported out of the complicated world of polytheism (many gods), where even the gods themselves are part of the physical universe, into the stunningly simple universe where one God is responsible for everything, and where he himself is not part of creation at all—not a "fairy at the bottom of the garden" or a "flying spaghetti monster," but the *ground* of all existence.

Here is perhaps the most basic misunderstanding perpetuated by recent popular literature on atheism. The "god" Richard Dawkins and others debunk is *part* of the universe, an object that ought to be observable, like a wall in a house or an actor in a play. Dawkins' supposedly knockdown argument against God reveals his mistake. He insists that any god capable of developing a complex universe would himself have to be more highly developed and complex than the universe. This in turn—so his logic goes—begs the question: How did god's own complexity develop? Dawkins' case against the Creator, in other words, boils down to the old chestnut *who-made-god?* But as many philosophers (including atheist ones) have pointed out to Dawkins, this is a weak argument from an otherwise highly educated man.

Philosophy textbooks routinely emphasize that classical theism — the kind we're talking about here — concerns a Being *beyond time and space.* It is precisely the observation that everything that exists in the universe *is caused by something else*, which leads to the philosophical affirmation that the ultimate cause of the universe must, of necessity and by definition, be timeless and nonspatial. This Being, therefore, cannot be *preceded* by anything, nor can it have *developed*; it cannot be *part* of the physical universe at all. As British intellectual Francis Spufford recently quipped:

> When people who believe in God talk about God, we don't mean that a being exists who is an animal like ourselves, only bigger and cleverer and more complex. We don't think He lives in the universe. In fact we don't think that He exists in any environment; we don't imagine that He had to grow, or evolve, or appear, or emerge, thanks to some process or other. It's the other way up. We think that all processes exist thanks to Him; we think that He is the universe's environment. We may well be wrong, crazed, doolally, travelling first-class on the delusion express, but showing that God-the-evolved-organism is unlikely says nothing about the probability of the different thing we do in fact believe. Arguing with people imposes an unfortunate necessity to find out what they think before you open your big mouth to contradict it. (Francis Spufford,

Apologetic: How, Despite Everything, Christianity Can Make Surprising Emotional Sense [HarperOne, 2013], 68–69)

God is not an actor within a play, to recall that image; he is its Director. He cannot be seen as a figure in the work, but his majesty and creativity are seen in every hint of rational order throughout the universe. This is the God of Genesis 1, in contrast to the gods of *Enuma Elish*.

BOOK NOTES

For philosophically minded readers, I would recommend one recent book that powerfully lays out the difference between "classical theism" and the "flying spaghetti monster" versions of god targeted by the New Atheism: David Bentley Hart, *The Experience of God* (Yale University Press, 2013).

The difference between Genesis 1 and *Enuma Elish* can also be seen in what each says about creation itself. In the Babylonian story the creation was a result of a haphazard war. Genesis says it is a work of art. Scholars point out a clear fourfold pattern in Genesis 1. Each creative scene (1) commences with a simple command, (2) tells of the fulfillment of the command, (3) includes an elaboration of the command, and (4) concludes with the day formula, "there was evening, there was morning." The first paragraph sets up the pattern for the rest of the chapter:

> [*1. Command*] And God said, "Let there be light," and [*2. Fulfillment*] there was light. [*3. Elaboration*] God saw that the light was good, and he separated the light from the darkness. God called the light "day," and the darkness

he called "night." [*4. Conclusion*] And there was evening, and there was morning—the first day. (Genesis 1:3–5)

The literary effect of this structure is to underline that the creation is the result of an orderly mind. This is far from the ancient view that creation was accidental and haphazard. I hardly need to point out that this ancient biblical view has been vindicated time and time again in the history of modern physics, which underlines for us the extraordinary orderliness of the universe.

For a measured account of this orderliness and its theological implications by a top flight physicist, who also knows a bit about theology, see Stephen Barr, *Modern Physics and Ancient Faith* (University of Notre Dame Press, 2003).

BOOK NOTES

The next big idea in *Enuma Elish* is that humans are merely an afterthought, designed only to serve the gods, to feed them. To be created out of the blood of the losing god (Kinju) is to exist at the bottom rung of the hierarchical ladder. A similar thought is found in the ancient Akkadian "Myth of Atrahasis," where the ghost of a slain god was deposited in human flesh. The *Encyclopedia Britannica* describes well the effects of this ancient Mesopotamian belief system on their anthropology:

> About human destiny all sources agree. However they may have come into being, human beings were meant to toil in order to provide food, clothing, housing, and service for the gods, so that they, relieved of all manual

labour, could live the life of a governing upper class, a landed nobility. In the scheme of existence humanity was thus never an end, always just a means. ("Mesopotamian Religion," Encyclopædia Britannica [Encyclopaedia Britannica Ultimate Reference Suite, 2010])

Genesis has a radically different view of humanity. Men and women are created in the sixth scene, on the sixth day, not as an afterthought but as the climax of the narrative, and they are made not just to serve the gods — or the God — but to bear his image:

> Then God said, "Let us make mankind in our image, in our likeness, so that they may rule over the fish in the sea and the birds in the sky, over the livestock and all the wild animals, and over all the creatures that move along the ground."
> So God created mankind in his own image, in the image of God he created them; male and female he created them. (Genesis 1:26–27)

The expression "image of God" has had a profound influence on the Western understanding of the value of humankind. It means that men and women (and notice it is both man and woman) stand in a *filial* relationship to God; they are his offspring, as it were. They bear the family resemblance. There have been several attempts to "locate" this image in some ability within *homo sapiens* — our moral sense, perhaps, or our capacity for rational thought — but it is probably best to think of it more as a divine "commission," which every person possesses regardless of capabilities. God *considers* us his offspring and grants us the mission of "ruling" the world on his behalf (NB: If God is a loving Father, then "rule" here does not mean *plunder* but *lead* for good ends, just as God himself leads his people). The notion that everyone, whether rich or poor, strong or weak, educated or not, bears the divine image has inspired the long Western tradition, unknown in pagan history, of regarding human beings as inalienably precious whatever their utility in the world.

Nicholas Wolterstorff of Yale University has written a terrific book outlining the history of human rights and their philosophical roots in the biblical notion that humans are made in God's image: *Justice: Rights and Wrongs* (Princeton University Press, 2010).

BOOK NOTES

Finally, *Enuma Elish* says that nature, the physical stuff of the world, is secondary, ephemeral, and accidental. It is the wreckage of a war. Genesis, on the other hand, says that creation is *very good*. To ancient ears this would have been puzzling, but the biblical writer says it *seven times* so that no reader will miss the point. Created stuff is good.

GENESIS VERSUS ATHEISM

The starting point of the biblical story is not creation's fall, but its glory. The starting point of the Christian worldview, therefore, is not the corruption of the world but its goodness, its sacredness. Christians believe that a good God created a good world in which he placed good people to do good work. This is a million miles from *Enuma Elish*, with its accidental creation and capricious deities.

The claims of Genesis are also a million miles from the modern evolutionary story with its equally accidental world. I am not disputing the science that says that complex organisms evolved from simple ones through a process of the selection of traits suited to survival. However, I do dispute the worldview that says the whole thing was blind, accidental, and totally haphazard. Such a claim does not arise directly from the science; it is a metaphysical interpretation of the data, and it is one the Bible rejects (claiming instead that God imprinted his orderliness of creation).

Indeed, the modern evolutionary story is probably not even good science. One of the world's premier evolutionary scientists, specializing in the emergence of life or Evolutionary Palaeobiology, is Simon Conway Morris of the University of Cambridge in the UK. He shows that, while there is an unimaginably large number of possible evolutionary pathways for organisms, "nature" tends to impose an extraordinarily narrow field of solutions to evolutionary problems. The result is that biological structures (like the capacity to produce silken threads, the eye, features of cacti) evolve in similar ways *completely independently* of each other. His claim is not that God intervenes to make these similar mutations. His point is that there is a basic order imposed on the universe that makes organisms not just possible but *inevitable*—even those strange organisms that have developed minds to understand such things! I don't know enough about this subject to pontificate about these things, but I can say that this viewpoint, known as "convergence," has gained widespread acceptance among evolutionary specialists.

An evolutionary worldview may not lead to superstition, as *Enuma Elish* did, but it will lead to relativism, because there are no absolute values, only the values you decide to assign to things. It will also lead, if you follow its logic through, to nihilism, a loss of absolute meaning, because there is no inherent significance to the accidental organisms of the world, only the significance you choose to attach to them.

It is ironic to me that atheists, particularly recently, have been arguing that the biblical worldview is the enemy of *the good*—that it is stultifying, life-denying, and inhibiting. Michel Onfray, a professor of philosophy in France, writes in his book *The Atheist Manifesto*:

> The religion of the one God espouses these [life-denying] impulses. It seeks to promote self-hatred to the detriment of the body, to discredit the intelligence, to despise the flesh, and to prize everything that stands in the way of a gratified subjectivity. Launched against others, it foments contempt. (Michel Onfray, *The Atheist Manifesto* [Arcade Publishing, 2005], 67)

I have no doubt that throughout history there have indeed been Christians who mirror Onfray's unhappy type. But it is a misreading of history to say that this was in any way typical. It is an even worse misreading of theology to say that the biblical worldview itself promotes such a negative view of life. The shoe is surely on the other foot. How can a cogent atheistic argument be made for the inherent goodness or worth of creation, when the starting point and the end point are accidental?

The difference between the atheistic (or pagan) viewpoint and the biblical viewpoint is the difference between viewing life as an accident and viewing it as a work of art. Two people could look at the Jackson Pollock painting *No.5 1948* with totally different perspectives. One might look at the work and declare it "an accident" (at first glance, this particular painting could be mistaken for an accident in a paint factory! Google it.). Another, however, could inspect it closely and recognize the subtle beauty and intention of the piece for what it is — one of the most expensive pieces of artwork ever sold (US $140 million). Obviously, the approach of the two art inspectors toward the piece would not be the same. How one cares for (what one considers) a sheet of fiberboard with scribble on it and how one cares for a Pollock painting could hardly be more different.

The difference between the pagan/atheist view of existence and the biblical view of existence is enormous. If you know the world to be beautifully designed and intentionally created — that is, if you see the genius behind it — you have a logical and moral imperative to treat it with reverence and care. Of course, both atheists and Christians can be equally cruel or kind toward the world. But only for the Christian (and, of course, our Jewish friends) is care of the world a *necessary corollary* of a worldview.

Bestselling psychologist and social commentator Hugh Mackay argues that the number one need of human beings is "to be taken seriously." Knowing we are valuable, his research indicates, trumps all other felt needs (beyond basic necessities, of course). While not written from a Christian viewpoint, his recent *What Makes Us Tick? The Ten Desires That Drive Us* (Hachette, 2013), I think, underlines the need in our day to recover the biblical view of creation and of humanity made in the image of God. Nothing in a secular worldview can compete with the *seriousness* with which the Bible looks upon the world and its men and women. The inimitable C. S. Lewis, Oxford and Cambridge don and author of the timeless Narnia books, put it provocatively:

> There are no ordinary people. You have never talked to a mere mortal. Nations, cultures, arts and civilizations—these are mortal. But it is immortals whom we joke with, work with, marry, snub, and exploit. This does not mean that we are to be perpetually solemn. We must play. But our merriment must be of that kind (and it is, in fact, the merriest kind) which exists between people who have, from the outset, taken each other seriously. And our charity must be a real and costly love, with deep feeling for the sins in spite of which we love the sinner. Next to the Blessed Sacrament itself [he means the bread and wine of Communion], your neighbour is the holiest object presented to your senses. (*The Weight of Glory* [HarperOne, 2009], 46)

I can't prove any of this is true. As I have said, this is not that sort of book, anyway. However, I think it is clear that if these biblical ideas are true—if the universe is intended, ordered, and kindly mindful of us—it will make a world of difference to our lives.

2

WHY SO MUCH IS BAD: ADAM'S STORY AND OURS

"CURSED IS THE GROUND BECAUSE OF YOU."

(GENESIS 3:17)

The Christian vision of life is grounded in the idea that the world is a good creation — it is the intentional, deliberate artwork of an orderly, loving God. Our experiences bear this out. We see the threads of beauty woven into the fabric of our existence.

But, of course, this is a patchwork world. There are threads of disaster, disease, and heartbreak, too. Here is another truth of the biblical narrative: a dark thread runs not only through the world, but through the very heart of humanity. These glorious creatures are also rebels and sinners. The seventeenth-century French mathematician, physicist, and philosopher Blaise Pascal put it like this: "What sort of freak then, is man! How novel, monstrous, how chaotic, how paradoxical, how prodigious! Judge of all things, feeble earthworm, repository of truth, sink of doubt and error, glory and refuse of the universe!" (Blaise Pascal, *Pensées* [trans. A. J. Krailsheimer; New York: Penguin, 1966], VII. Contradictions, section 131, 66).

Two hundred years later, the great German philosopher and atheist Friedrich Nietzsche despised Christianity for putting such an awful idea in the head of so great an intellect as Pascal: "the most deplorable example," Nietzsche wrote in the aptly titled *Anti-Christ*, is "the depraving of Pascal, who believed his reason had been depraved by original sin while it had only been depraved by his Christianity" (Friedrich Nietzsche, *Twilight of Idols / The Anti-Christ* [Penguin Books, 1990], 129). It is one of the most confronting ideas of the Bible, yet it is one that illuminates as much as disturbs: God's glorious creatures are profoundly fallen.

Christians call this chaotic feebleness "sin." It is a deeply unfashionable term. On the one hand, it is sometimes stripped of its meaning and power, as when "sinfulness" means nothing more than a cheeky tendency to overindulge in ice cream or chocolate. On the other hand, for some the word "sin" brings to mind a pulpit-thumping, fire-breathing preacher who wants to crush people into an acceptance of their abject worthlessness. Either approach diminishes this key biblical concept.

Despite the unpopularity of the word "sin," the Bible's premise that humanity is the glory and refuse of the universe, as Pascal put it, does resonate. Nietzsche can decry the concept as much as he likes, but we see examples of this human paradox all around us.

Soon after the fall of the ruthless dictator Saddam Hussein, private photos were released that showed him as the doting grandfather of little ones who loved him. We read stories about people who act with great courage and seeming altruism who become corrupted or act terribly toward their families in private. I am writing this particular chapter in a hotel room in America as CNN offers seemingly endless coverage of the moral "fall" of the great General David Petraeus, war hero and (now former) head of the Central Intelligence Agency. If we are honest with ourselves, most will acknowledge a similar paradox in our day-to-day lives. We love our children intensely, give generously to charity, or work hard for little thanks. But then there are moments when we lose our temper (toward these loved ones), speak words that wound or deceive, and find ourselves selfishly neglecting the plight of the poor. We are confronted with the dark and selfish twist to the human heart.

The Bible opens, as we have seen, with a story about the manifest goodness and beauty of the world. The next story, however, explains the wicked, the wretched, the dark streak in humanity. It is the story of the fall. It is such a classic narrative, I feel I should quote it at length:

> The LORD God took the man and put him in the Garden of Eden to work it and take care of it. And the LORD God commanded the man, "You are free to eat from any tree in the garden; but you must not eat from the tree of the knowledge of good and evil, for when you eat from it you will certainly die." ...
>
> Now the serpent was more crafty than any of the wild animals the LORD God had made. He said to the woman, "Did God really say, 'You must not eat from any tree in the garden'?"

The woman said to the serpent, "We may eat fruit from the trees in the garden, but God did say, 'You must not eat fruit from the tree that is in the middle of the garden, and you must not touch it, or you will die.'"

"You will not certainly die," the serpent said to the woman. "For God knows that when you eat from it your eyes will be opened, and you will be like God, knowing good and evil."

When the woman saw that the fruit of the tree was good for food and pleasing to the eye, and also desirable for gaining wisdom, she took some and ate it. She also gave some to her husband, who was with her, and he ate it. Then the eyes of both of them were opened, and they realized they were naked; so they sewed fig leaves together and made coverings for themselves. Then the man and his wife heard the sound of the LORD God as he was walking in the garden in the cool of the day, and they hid from the LORD God among the trees of the garden. But the LORD God called to the man, "Where are you?"

He answered, "I heard you in the garden, and I was afraid because I was naked; so I hid."

And he said, "Who told you that you were naked? Have you eaten from the tree that I commanded you not to eat from?"

The man said, "The woman you put here with me— she gave me some fruit from the tree, and I ate it."

Then the LORD God said to the woman, "What is this you have done?"

The woman said, "The serpent deceived me, and I ate." (Genesis 2:15 – 3:13)

The story begins with God bestowing on Adam and Eve authority and immense freedom. They are made in the "image of God" and are told to rule over the whole world. God tells them that they may eat from any tree in the garden of Eden, except one—the tree of the knowledge of good and evil.

The word "knowledge" used here is derived from the Hebrew word *yada* (from where, I suppose, the all-knowing Star Wars character Yoda gets his name). But the word has a flexible meaning. It can mean "to experience," "to choose," "to determine," and, on occasion, "to have sex"—hence the expression "to know a woman in the biblical sense."

Many scholars suggest that "knowledge," as it is used in Genesis 2:17, has the nuance of "to determine." This is the tree of the *determination* of good and evil. It is not that God does not want Adam to know the difference between good and evil; that wouldn't make sense of the narrative, in any case, since God's command not to eat from this particular tree presupposes that Adam was able to comprehend that it would be wrong to go against God's wishes. The real point seems to be that God does not want Adam to imagine that he is free to choose what is good and what is evil. That prerogative belongs to God alone.

When Adam takes a piece of fruit from the tree of the knowledge of good and evil, it is an act of defiance that usurps God's authority to reveal—as the reflection of his own character—what is right and what is wrong. To be clear, the Bible does not say that things are right or wrong only because God says so (as if good and bad are arbitrary categories of God's preferences). Philosophers have heavily critiqued such a "divine command theory" of ethics. But nor is it the case that there is some external moral law under which God himself sits, so that even God is constrained to obey objective precepts. The biblical way of thinking says that God himself is "the Good," and that he ordered the world as a reflection of his own good character. As a result, that which God commands and that which is inherently good are one and the same. Whatever moral law there is in the universe is simply a reflection of his own nature. To defy God, as Adam did, is to defy the Good.

When Adam and Eve defied God, according to Genesis 3, everything promptly falls apart — socially, physically, and spiritually. This threefold pattern is crucial to the unfolding biblical narrative.

Socially, their relationship with one another, which was previously full of intimacy and joy, is now filled with blame and embarrassment.

The *physical* dimension collapses too. The land, which previously provided easily and abundantly for Adam and Eve's needs, is now difficult and becomes a place of enmity with humanity. God says to Adam: "Cursed is the ground because of you; through painful toil you will eat food from it all the days of your life."

Most profoundly, Adam and Eve's *spiritual* relationships, their relationships with God, are now fractured. Before Adam and Eve sinned, Genesis offers a picture of the Creator and human beings in fellowship in the garden together. However, after they eat the fruit, God comes walking through the garden, and, in a poignant and disturbing scene, Adam and Eve hide from their Maker. We are probably right to detect some "comedy" here, a tragic irony that humans would imagine they could hide from the omniscient Lord of the world! How much of life involves a petty hiding from the Almighty!

When God told Adam and Eve not to eat from the tree of the knowledge of good and evil, he said that the consequence for doing so would be death. While Adam and Eve did eventually die, before they died, they saw the breakdown of their spiritual relationship, social relationships, and relationship with the physical environment. This is *true death*—the destruction of that which is good in the created world, that for which we were made.

INTERPRETATIONS OF THE TEXT

It is worth noting that the Adam and Eve narrative has been interpreted in different ways. Some people, a large number, read Adam as a *historical individual* and the story as a *straightforward piece of history.* They believe he was a real historical man who met a real talking snake and ate a real piece of fruit.

Others see Adam merely as a *symbol of humanity.* People who hold this view point out that the language of Genesis 3 is unlike the language of historical narrative; it is far more "literary" than other sections of the Bible. They point out that talking snakes and trees with names—the tree of life, the tree of the knowledge of good and evil—look like literary devices. They sound like they are meant to be read as metaphors. Most of all, people point out that the word "Adam" is not really a name. It has become one, of course, but in ancient times it was the Hebrew word for *human being.* Adam is the Hebrew Everyman.

The third interpretation of the Adam story sees Adam as

a *symbol of Israel*, and hence they see his story as a deliberate anticipation of the entire Old Testament story. Israel would later be given a promised land, a beautiful garden, and a law to obey (these events are told in the books of Deuteronomy, Joshua, Judges, and so on). When Israel does not obey, when they are led astray by the Canaanites, one of whose famous gods was the serpent, they are expelled from the land (as told in the books of 1 and 2 Kings). A great many scholars see the Genesis 3 narrative as a specific anticipation of what is to come in the rest of the Old Testament.

The fourth interpretation, and the one I find most convincing, sees Adam as a *concrete symbol*. This view agrees that Adam is a symbol of humanity and of Israel, but maintains that the narrative speaks of a *real event*, albeit in obvious picture language. On this view, there was a time in this world when a prehistoric individual or couple was in perfect communion with God and then in some way defied God. This story is now told in a highly symbolic way as the story of the Israelites and the story of all of humanity.

BOOK NOTES

An important recent book explores the variety of views of Adam (in different terminology from my own) in full conversation with evolutionary science: Matthew Barrett and Ardel B. Caneday, eds., *Four Views of the Historical Adam* (Zondervan, 2013).

Whichever interpretation you find most compelling, the central point of the narrative is clear: the Adam and Eve story is *our* story. It is the story of all humanity.

THE MYTH OF PROGRESS

I sometimes wonder if the "evolutionary" view of life so common today makes it difficult for some of us to believe the biblical teaching on human sinfulness, that we are all "Adam." I am not talking specifically about biological evolution—though the popularity of the theory no doubt perpetuates the problem—but rather the unquestioned assumption of "progress" in all things. We look at advances in medicine and technology and extrapolate to society's opinions about other important things, such as meaning and, in particular, ethics. Because I can put 10,000 songs on my iPod and watch endless videos on my iPad, any society that could produce such wonders must be some kind of pinnacle of human achievement.

Almost by definition today, the old is inferior to the new. Our culture has invented powerful boo-words that dispense with the traditions of the past in an instant. When my skeptical friends call my Christian views "dated," "antiquated," or "medieval," they imagine there is no more arguing to be done. And what could be more medieval than the notion of "sin"!

I admit there have been plenty of advances in the last two hundred years. Leaving aside the obvious medical and technological leaps-forward, we can point to the abolition of slavery as evidence of progress. The demise of racial discrimination is another example, as is the increasing rights of women. Yet, even here, things are not clear-cut if you take a two-thousand-year view. As early as the fifth-century, Saint Augustine tells us, Christians were conducting regular raids to free slaves from the slave-trading ships, feeding them, and secreting them on their way. Moreover, the racial problems in Western society were not the continuation of a Christian tradition gratefully overturned in twentieth-century secularism. They were, in fact, a recent aberration in the history of the West. Discrimination between light- and dark-skinned peoples was not nearly so prominent in first-century Greece or Rome, and within Christian communities of the period, such racism was virtually nonexistent. The modern Civil Rights Movement was more a recovery of an ancient Christian tradition than an example of recent human progress.

Then there are all the ways in which contemporary society is worse than older societies. There are things happening today that would have been virtually unthinkable in, say, medieval times or ancient Christendom. Nearly half of all marriages fail, and half of these involve children. Whatever one's view on divorce, these statistics are a disaster for Western society. Again, charitable giving as a proportion of income is actually falling, at least in Australia (I don't have the international figures). And the rich give away less in percentage terms than the poor—which suggests that economic advancement is hardly "progress." Add to this list the horrific fact that a million girls and women are trafficked each year for sex (UN Global Initiative to Fight Human Trafficking, Fact Sheet), and the top destination countries include Japan, Belgium, Netherlands, Germany, and the US—the seemingly "advanced" countries.

Terry Eagleton, a leading public intellectual in Britain and distinguished professor of English literature at the University of Lancaster, rightly challenges the modern myth that everything is getting better; he reserves his harshest criticism for the New Atheists:

> Today, ironically, a mindless progressivism poses a greater threat to political change than an awareness of the night-mare of history. The true antirealists are those like the scientist Richard Dawkins, with his staggeringly com-placent belief that we are all becoming kinder and more civilised. It is true that some things get better in some respects. But some things also get worse. And of these the dewy-eyed Dawkins has scarcely anything to say. Nobody would gather from his smug account of the evolving wis-dom of humanity that we are also faced with planetary devastation, the threat of nuclear conflict, the spreading catastrophe of AIDS and other deadly viruses, neoimpe-rial zealotry, mass migrations of the dispossessed, politi-cal fanaticism and a reversion to Victorian-type economic inequalities. (Terry Eagleton, *On Evil* [Yale University Press, 2010], 155–56)

Eagleton does not describe himself as a Christian believer, but he admits in this same book to a certain attraction to the biblical notions of "original sin" and "radical evil."

THE PRACTICAL PRINCIPLE OF SIN

The story of Adam and Eve, or the principle of human sinful-ness that springs from it, is a key way that Christians make sense of the evil and darkness in the world. It's an idea that shapes everything, including Christian anthropology. The expectation is that people, all of us, are sinful. This might seem depressing, as Nietzsche certainly suggested, but there is also a liberating realism in believing we are *fundamentally glorious* and *fundamentally wretched* at the same time.

I have often thought it would be a terrible burden to think we are good through-and-through. How could we live with the perpetual disappointment of daily evidence to the contrary? But a doctrine of sin liberates us from these expectations. I am "Adam"; you are "Adam." This is not to say that Christians become comfortable with their sins, but they do begin to see through the fantasy of imagining we are deeply and inherently good. And that realization brings a peace.

Coming to terms with sin is not unlike coming to terms with middle age—a theme I have had on my mind in recent years. In a tennis match a year or so ago, I came face to face with the awkward reality that I am no longer twenty years of age. In my mind, I was a young man on that court. The body saw it differently. When I badly missed a point I was sure I could win, I stood there puzzled and deflated for a good thirty seconds, wondering how I could possibly have missed the shot. In a flash of clarity, it dawned on me: my twenty-year-old imaginings were face-to-face with the forty-something realities. Oddly, the realization was liberating—and the game of tennis improved! I doubt this is a perfect analogy but it highlights something real. To not accept our flawed human nature, to resist the notion of sin, is to live in a fantasy in the court of life and will inevitably confuse and deflate.

Accepting the doctrine of human sinfulness should also remove any basis for judgmentalism. Some Christians have an unfortunate reputation for judgmentalism. It is unfortunate, not simply because it costs Christians in the popularity stakes, but because the Christian teaching on sin (not even starting on the teaching about love and forgiveness) assumes *universal* sinfulness. Instantly, the basis for condemning someone else evaporates. British intellectual and reluctant convert to Christianity Francis Spufford puts all this provocatively in his recent *Apologetic: How, Despite Everything, Christianity Can Make Surprising Emotional Sense:*

> So of all things, Christianity isn't supposed to be about gathering up the good people (shiny! happy! squeaky clean!) and excluding the bad people (frightening! alien! repulsive!) for the very simple reason that there aren't any good people. Not that can be securely designated as such. It can't be about circling the wagons of virtue out in the suburbs and keeping the unruly inner city at bay. This, I realize, goes flat contrary to the present predominant image of it as something existing in prissy, fastidious little enclaves, far from life's messier zones and inclined to get all "judgmental" about them. Again, of course, there are Christians like that.... The religion certainly can slip into being a club or a cosy affinity group or a wall against the world. But it isn't supposed to be. What it's supposed to be is a league of the guilty. Not all guilty of the same things, or in the same way, or to the same degree, but enough for us to recognize each other. (Frances Spufford, *Apologetic: How, Despite Everything, Christianity Can Make Surprising Emotional Sense* [HarperOne, 2013], 46–47)

Accepting the unpopular notions of human "sinfulness" also leads to a life of thankfulness. To offer an illustration: when my son was twelve, we were at the beach near Sydney and he got caught in what we call a "rip"—a dangerous beach current—that was quickly dragging him out to sea. Josh is a pretty good swimmer, but it was clear that he was in trouble. As that realization came upon me, a surf life-saver ran past me, dived through the waves out to Josh, and dragged him back to safety. We were very relieved, and in our minds the lifesaver was a hero. Josh's first words, how-ever, were not "thank you," but "I was fine, I was fine." He was nowhere close to being fine. But because he did not understand his dangerous predicament, he had little sense of thankfulness. The Christian life is lived with a profound sense of "sinfulness" that leads to an even deeper sense of thankfulness to God for his mercy. A life of thankfulness permeates the biblical view of human existence, from the Old Testament to (especially) the New Testament. It moti-vates ethics and inspires worship. But more about that later.

EAST OF EDEN

John Steinbeck's novel *East of Eden* (Viking Press, 1952; Penguin Books, 2002) uses this expression to denote not only physical dislocation from paradise but the progres-sive falling apart of things. This idea of a fall from grace at break-neck speed comes, of course, from these opening chapters of the Bible, as Adam and Eve are ejected from the garden for their disobedience and so are banished *east of Eden*. In the chilling imagery of the climactic verses of the account of the fall we read: "After he drove the man out, he placed on the *east side* of the Garden of Eden cherubim and a flaming sword flashing back and forth to guard the way to the tree of life" (Genesis 3:24, italics added). This "eastward" journey becomes something of a motif, repeated again in Genesis 11:2.

The life of the human race from that moment on is a story of rapidly escalating evil and suffering. In Genesis 4, Adam and Eve's son Cain murders his brother Abel out of jealousy. This trajectory continues—as humanity continues to march "east of Eden"—to the point where we read, "The LORD saw how great the wickedness of the human race had become on the earth" (Genesis 6:5). The famous flood narrative follows this statement, in which Noah and his family are rescued from the judgment falling on the earth. Noah's family becomes a powerful reminder to readers of Genesis that God's desire is to save rather than to destroy.

Many ancient cultures have a flood story—a point that probably hints at a real event in the deep past—but only Genesis casts this as a genuine judgment for sin. In the most famous alternative flood story, the *Epic of Atrahasis*, which predates the book of Genesis, the reason for the flood is the general annoyance that humanity had caused the gods: "for people were constantly disturbing them with their troubles, demands, and requests." Genesis also emphasizes that God longed to save Noah, his family, and the animals from his judgment, whereas in Mesopotamian accounts "the plan of the gods was that no one should survive"—and no one would have if the gods' secret plan had not slipped out (John Walton, ed., *Zondervan Illustrated Bible Backgrounds Commentary* [Zondervan, 2009], 1:49).

The tragic journey east of Eden continues into the climactic story of Genesis 1–11, the account of the Tower of

Babel, in which the people of the world decide to build a giant tower as a declaration of human autonomy from God. The narrative is introduced with the words, "As people moved *eastward*, they found a plain in Shinar and settled there" (Genesis 11:2, italics added). The account of the building of a monument to humanity's freedom from God has echoes of the original actions of Adam and Eve in seeking to determine for themselves, apart from the Creator, what is good and evil. It is a fitting climax to the first eleven chapters of the Bible, which, from a literary point of view, are a "pre-history" designed to set up the *actual history* of God's dealings with Israel, which begins in Genesis 12 (see next chapter).

The point we are meant to reflect on as we reach this sad climax is that without God's gracious intervention, humanity is on a spiral of self-absorption, injustice, and arrogance that will lead to humanity's ultimate fall. We will continue moving east of Eden. It is a point made eloquently by Malcolm Muggeridge, the great British journalist and intellectual, in a famous speech in Lausanne in 1974 to church leaders from around the world:

> Confronting the scene, it is, I confess, sometimes difficult to resist the conclusion, that Western man has decided to abolish himself, creating his own boredom out of his own affluence, his own vulnerability out of his own strength, his own impotence out of his own erotomania; himself blowing the trumpet that brings down the walls of his own city, and having convinced himself that he's too numerous, laboring with pill and scalpel and syringe to make himself fewer, until at last, having educated himself

into imbecility, and polluted and drugged himself into stupefaction, he keels over, a weary battered old Brontosaurus, and becomes extinct. Here I speak with some feeling, since it is through a realisation of the fantasies of power that I've come to recognise the irresistible truth of the Gospel of love that Jesus came into the world to expound. (Transcribed from a recording of "Living Through an Apocalypse," a speech of Malcolm Muggeridge at the Lausanne Conference on World Evangelization, 1974.)

But this is only part of the biblical story. Before humanity travels too far "east," God intervenes. He chooses an individual, from whom would come an entire nation. This nation would be the vehicle of his good intentions toward *all* nations. Enter: Abraham.

3

LIFE IN THREE DIMENSIONS: THE BLESSINGS OF FATHER ABRAHAM

"GO ... TO THE LAND I WILL SHOW YOU. I WILL MAKE YOU INTO A GREAT NATION, AND I WILL BLESS YOU."

(GENESIS 12:1–2)

The figure of Abraham is revered by Jews, Christians, and Muslims as a kind of "father" of faith—and rightly so, as we will see. Originally named Abram, he lived in southern Mesopotamia around 1900 BC—though some scholars place him slightly earlier. After God approached Abram and made promises to him, God changed his name to Abraham, which means "father of many nations." God made important promises to Abraham, which would shape Israel's relationship with God for centuries. It is no stretch to say that the divine pledge to this man captures all that the Bible holds out for humanity.

Imperial Rome saw Emperor Augustus as *Pater Patriae*, "Father of the Fatherland." I guess North Americans think of George Washington or Abraham Lincoln in this way.

We don't have a comparable figure where I come from — Aussies are more likely to boast, with a kind of inverted snobbery, about descending from First Fleet convicts! In any case, Abraham has a significance in the Bible that eclipses any national father figure; yet, curiously, his origins are as inglorious as any of the criminals that stepped onto Australian shores in 1788.

It is impossible to exaggerate the significance of the promises made to Abraham. Miss these and we miss the key that unlocks the Bible. These pledges are literally the answer to the problems raised in Genesis 1–11, and they provide a road map to the rest of the biblical narrative. Even today Abraham's faith forms the structure of Christian belief, practice, and hope.

God's promises to Abraham mark the reversal of the three diminishing elements of human existence mentioned in the previous chapter: the search for God (the *spiritual* element), relationships with one another (the *social* element), and connection to the environment itself (the *physical* element). All three dimensions are found in a single paragraph at the beginning of the Abraham narrative:

> The LORD had said to Abram, "Go from your country, your people and your father's household to the land I will show you.
>
> "I will make you into a great nation,
>   and I will bless you;
> I will make your name great,
>   and you will be a blessing.
> I will bless those who bless you,
>   and whoever curses you I will curse;

> and all peoples on earth
>> will be blessed through you."
>
> So Abram went, as the LORD had told him.
> (Genesis 12:1–4)

The paragraph is deceptively simple and sets the framework for belief in both the Old and New Testaments.

SPIRITUAL RESTORATION

Abraham is the archetype of relationship with God. He is a recipient of God's pure grace. Nothing in this crucial biblical text indicates that Abraham was a righteous or obedient man when God first approached him. We know from the preceding chapters that the whole world is scattered, the whole world is pagan, including Abraham. Then the Lord comes down and makes these incredible promises to him. God simply confronts Abraham with blessings he does not deserve, and Abraham to his credit responds to this grace with obedience.

This structure of relationship with God — grace first, then obedience — weaves its way through the entire Bible. It is both humbling and comforting. Even the great patriarch, the father of Israel, was not chosen for his goodness, and neither, so goes the Christian story, is *anyone*. He was a pagan from southern Mesopotamia, and God called him into a relationship grounded in grace, and out of that grace came Abraham's willingness to obey, described in the following lines: "So Abram went, as the LORD had told him.... There he built an altar to the LORD and called on the name of the LORD" (Genesis 12:4–8).

The same point is emphasized a few chapters later in Genesis when God enters into a "covenant" with Abraham. This is an important concept. Usually, covenants involved the declaration of promises and duties for *both* parties. It was a way for individuals, tribes, or nations to bind themselves to each other for some mutual benefit. However, when God formalizes his promise to Abraham, he makes a covenant that seems one-sided: the Creator binds himself in absolute terms to do good to Abraham. The following narrative is definitely odd to modern ears and also extraordinary in an ancient covenant-making context. An animal is killed and cut in two. The maker of the covenant walks through the middle of the carcass, as if to say, "If I break my covenant promise, may I end up like this slain animal." Curiously, however, it is God alone who participates in the ritual, thereby calling down a curse on himself if he does not fulfill his promise:

> So the LORD said to him, "Bring me a heifer, a goat and a ram, each three years old, along with a dove and a young pigeon."
>
> Abram brought all these to him, cut them in two and arranged the halves opposite each other; the birds, however, he did not cut in half. Then birds of prey came down on the carcasses, but Abram drove them away.
>
> As the sun was setting, Abram fell into a deep sleep, and a thick and dreadful darkness came over him.... When the sun had set and darkness had fallen, a smoking firepot with a blazing torch appeared and passed between the pieces. On that day the LORD made a covenant with Abram and said, "To your descendants I give this land, from the Wadi of Egypt to the great river, the Euphrates—the land of the Kenites, Kenizzites, Kadmonites,

Hittites, Perizzites, Rephaites, Amorites, Canaanites, Girgashites and Jebusites." (Genesis 15:9–21)

This notion of *covenant* is important for the biblical narrative. Indeed, it holds the story together. God makes promises to his people and calls on them to respond with faith. This covenant with Abraham—to bless him, to give him land, and to build him into a community that would bless the world—is where the entire biblical narrative is heading. The promises to Moses, to Israel, to King David, and so on are all outworkings of this covenant with Abraham. All of these promises reach their climax in the promises of Jesus Christ in the New Testament. The word *testament*, in fact, is just an old English word for "covenant." The Christian documents in the Bible are really just the documents of the "new covenant," the fulfillment of God's promises to Abraham.

None of this is to say that Abraham had no responsibilities to obey God. The point is that God's calling of Abraham and his covenant with him do not *depend* on a believer's behavior but on the Almighty's trustworthiness. Abraham did obey God, as the earlier passage makes clear (Genesis 12:4–8), but his actions were a response to divine favor, not the means of securing it.

Abraham's faith is the archetype of true faith. So, two thousand years later, Jesus uses the expression "son of Abraham" as shorthand for a sinner who has come to know God's mercy and favor. Jesus was going through Jericho on one occasion and met a prominent tax collector, a reviled figure in the first century, named Zacchaeus. Zacchaeus was overwhelmed by the kindness he encountered in Jesus and responded to that grace with a public statement of loyalty to Christ. Jesus declared, "This man, too, is a son of Abraham." For, he went on, "the Son of Man [that's Jesus] came to seek and to save the lost" (Luke 19:9–10). In other words, Abraham is the paradigmatic sinner startled by grace—lost but sought and saved. This is exactly how relationships with God are structured in Christianity, from the first book (Genesis) to the last book (Revelation). They are entirely grace-based and have nothing to do with merit or the particular goodness or badness of someone.

This has always been a favorite theme of Australians—perhaps because of their inglorious roots—even if institutional religion hasn't always conveyed the theme well. From our earliest convict days, Aussies have been drawn to Jesus Christ and his welcoming attitude toward "sinners." And the mistakes of churches don't seem to have dulled people's enthusiasm for him. While only about 15 percent of the country attends church semi-regularly (up to once a month), recent polls indicate high respect for, and even belief in, Jesus Christ: half of Australians (49 percent) think he was the most important figure in history; roughly the same number believe he rose from the dead (54 percent); and nearly three-quarters (75 percent) believe he performed miracles. All of this underlines the respect Australians have for Jesus, given that only 68 percent of them believe in any kind of "god" and just 63 percent believe miracles are even possible (sources: "Faith in Australia" [Nielsen Poll, 2009]; "Easter and Jesus" and "Here Comes Christmas—A National Representative Research-only Panel Survey" [McCrindle Research, March and December 2009]).

I am sure this secular affection for Jesus Christ stems

from his reputation as a man of deep spiritual grace, extending compassion to the immoral and irreligious. It's a theme that Jesus himself would have traced back to his own "father of the fatherland," when 1,800 years earlier Abraham was called by God in a sheer act of undeserved welcome. As I have said, this theme begins in Genesis, but it weaves its way through the entire biblical narrative.

If someone has spent most of their life in a Christian-influenced country, they may not appreciate how unique the theme of "grace" is in the religious landscape of the world. In Hinduism, for example, salvation does not come from grace, but as a reward for good behavior—if you follow the duties of your caste, you build up enough karma to merge with Brahman. It is similar in Buddhism. "Nirvana" in Buddhism does not come as a gift; rather, it comes as a reward at the end of following the eightfold path of the Buddha—right speech, right employment, right thought, and so on. In Islam, too, it is only by following the five pillars— the correct confession of faith, the five daily prayers, giving away 2.5 percent of your money, fasting during Ramadan, and visiting Mecca once in your life—that you can atone for sins and receive God's forgiveness.

BOOK NOTES | For readers wanting more information on the world religions and their various concepts of "salvation," I hope it's not presumptuous to suggest my own *Spectator's Guide to the World Religions* (Lion Hudson, 2008), in which I have tried my best to provide a fair account of each of the great faiths.

None of this is intended to critique the world's great faiths: maybe they're right and the Bible is wrong. I am just highlighting a significant difference between the religions of the world and biblical faith. The structure of relationship with God in a typical religious framework is: obedience first, favor second. The structure of relationship with God, found in the call of Abraham and then throughout the Bible, is: favor first, obedience second. I might repeat this theme once or twice before our tour through the Bible concludes!

SOCIAL RESTORATION

The promise to Abraham involved more than the renewal of the spiritual relationship. It was also about the restoration of humanity with each other, the *social* dimension. God is not just interested in connecting us with him, as if *private faith* is all that matters. True faith in God connects you to others.

In the promises to Abraham God reveals his intention to gather together a *nation*: "I will make you into a great nation" (Genesis 12:2). This is not a "chosen people" cut off from, or dominant over, the nations around it. The chosen people are meant to be a sign of renewed community and a vehicle of blessing to others, as the climactic words of the promise make clear: "All peoples on earth will be blessed through you." This is a golden thread of the Bible: Israel is chosen *in order to be a blessing to every other nation*. The selection of one nation was always designed to lead to the inclusion of every nation. In the story of Babel in Genesis 11, the nations were scattered. In the promise to Abraham here in Genesis 12, God makes plans to bring all people back together.

This theme weaves its way through the Old Testament, as God establishes the significant ancient people of Israel and as he brings them into contact with the surrounding people, some of whom embrace the blessing of Israel. But it comes to fulfillment only in the New Testament. Jesus lives, teaches, dies, and rises again, we are told, for all the world, not just for his fellow Israelites. The first-century apostle Paul, writing twenty years after Jesus, puts the New Testament perspective perfectly: "Understand, then, that those who have faith are children of Abraham. Scripture foresaw that God would justify the Gentiles [i.e., non-Israelites] by faith, and announced the gospel in advance to Abraham: 'All nations will be blessed through you.' So those who rely on faith are blessed along with Abraham, the man of faith" (Galatians 3:7–9).

This idea reaches its climax in the final book of the New Testament, Revelation, where a vision is given of people from all the earth gathered together because of Jesus (depicted here as the sacrificial lamb): "After this I looked, and there before me was a great multitude that no one could count, from every nation, tribe, people and language, standing before the throne and before the Lamb" (Revelation 7:9).

God's desire is to gather all people into a family. He is interested in both spiritual and social restoration. Today we take for granted that Christianity is an international, multicultural faith, one not bound to its Middle Eastern origins or to its recent Western expansion. In fact, on current trends "China is destined to become the largest Christian country in the world very soon," says Fenggang Yang, a professor of sociology at Purdue University and author of *Religion in China: Survival and Revival under Communist Rule* (Oxford University Press,

2012). In a recent interview, he predicts that by 2030 there will be more than 247 million Christians in what is still a formally atheistic nation (www.telegraph.co.uk/news/worldnews/asia/china/10776023/China-on-course-to-become-worlds-most-Christian-nation-within-15-years.html). Abraham could hardly have imagined the true import of the promise, "I will make you into a great nation ... and all peoples on earth will be blessed through you" (Genesis 12:2–3), but we continue to witness its fulfillment before our eyes today.

PHYSICAL RESTORATION

There is a third dimension to this all-important promise to Abraham. God told the patriarch, "Go from your country, your people and your father's household to the land I will show you" (Genesis 12:1). There is a physical or environmental aspect to God's plans through Abraham. As the narrative of Genesis unfolds, God later shows him a land, Canaan, and pledges that it would belong to his descendants. In a truly strange historical outcome, there are physical descendants of Abraham living there to this day, almost four thousand years later. It's what we call the modern state of Israel.

This "Promised Land" is central to the Old Testament story, but it's an idea that Christians don't always know what to do with. Some Christians become "Zionists," believing God has mandated those particular longitudes and latitudes known as Israel, or "Zion" in religious speak, for the Jewish people forever. While I believe you can make a sociopolitical argument for giving the harassed and persecuted Jewish people of post-WWII Europe a safe piece of land, Zionism is not theologically endorsed by the New Testament. Only a revision of history can deny that the state of Israel was established at the tragic expense of many thousands of Arabs—both Muslim and Christian—whose families had been living there for centuries. I love modern Israel and visit there regularly, but it saddens me that regaining this land cost many lives and continues to disturb many others. In my view—indeed, in the view of the vast majority of Christians throughout history—the Promised Land is no longer theologically significant at all. It stands only as a marvelous historical symbol of God's desire to restore the whole earth, to fulfill his *physical* purposes for humankind.

BOOK NOTES

It is so difficult to find a fair account of the history and politics of Israel and Palestine today, but one that is certainly designed to achieve this is the hundred-page gem in the *Oxford Very Short Introduction* series by Martin Bunton, *The Palestinian-Israeli Conflict* (Oxford University Press, 2013).

Most Christians, however, do not struggle with thinking that "land" is so important; they fall into the opposite trap of devaluing the physical world more generally. Christianity has long been influenced by what is sometimes called "Platonic" thinking, prizing the mind and spirit over physical matter. This has lots of negative outcomes. One is the assumption that, while God was committed to the earth in the Old Testament, he drops his interest in real estate entirely in the New Testament and becomes concerned only with "heavenly" things.

One of the members of my church, an architecture academic, told me recently about a conference he attended on sustainable environmental architecture. At the conference, one of the speakers said, "The whole problem that we have facing us in the environmental movement is Christians. They believe they're waiting for a kingdom to come. This allows them to rape and pillage the physical earth." My friend was horrified. I am sure there have been Christians in history who have believed this sort of thing, and the environment has suffered accordingly. But this is a blatant distortion of Christian belief.

God is deeply concerned with physical, earthly things. The world was created by him and declared to be "good." Part of his promise to Abraham, echoed time and again through the Old Testament, is the return of his people to the Promised Land. And in the New Testament, this promise of Eden recaptured, of a promised land, is not rescinded. It is *magnified*. According to the New Testament, the land of Eden and the land promised to Abraham find their ultimate expression in the renewal of *all* creation, not just those particular longitudes and latitudes. The Bible climaxes with the promise that *all creation* will be redeemed:

> For the creation waits in eager expectation for the children of God to be revealed. For the creation was subjected to frustration, not by its own choice, but by the will of the one who subjected it, in hope that the creation itself will be liberated from its bondage to decay and brought into the freedom and glory of the children of God. (Romans 8:19–21)

In keeping with his promise we are looking forward to a new heaven and a new earth, where righteousness dwells.

So then, dear friends, since you are looking forward to this, make every effort to be found spotless, blameless and at peace with him. (2 Peter 3:13–14)

Then I saw "a new heaven and a new earth," for the first heaven and the first earth had passed away, and there was no longer any sea. I saw the Holy City, the new Jerusalem, coming down out of heaven from God, prepared as a bride beautifully dressed for her husband. And I heard a loud voice from the throne saying, "Look! God's dwelling place is now among the people, and he will dwell with them. They will be his people, and God himself will be with them and be their God. 'He will wipe every tear from their eyes. There will be no more death' or mourning or crying or pain, for the old order of things has passed away."

He who was seated on the throne said, "I am making everything new!" (Revelation 21:1–5)

When Christians talk of "heaven," they mean something very different from the contemporary ethereal picture of spirits floating around in white robes, playing harps, sitting on clouds, and eating cream cheese. This is a strange, half-Platonic, half-Hollywood notion that looks nothing like the picture offered in the Bible.

If anything, this contemporary picture of heaven resembles the hopes of the Eastern faiths. Within Buddhism the great hope is Nirvana, which literally means "to be blown out." Nirvana is, in the teaching of Buddha, "the cessation of matter and sensation." And in Hinduism, the great problem *is* physical creation. *Moksha* or liberation is the deliverance of your soul, your *atman,* out of creation so you never have to come back into this physical reality.

But the hoped-for future presented in the Bible, as we will see in more detail in the final chapter of the book, is the restoration and re-creation of the physical world. It is an *earthy* picture, a heaven where we have real bodies; we eat, sing, drink wine, and enjoy the restored, resplendent environment. This is the ultimate Eden, the ultimate Promised Land.

Between starting and finishing this book, a dear elderly friend passed away after a long illness. Marie had been a French existentialist and intellectual atheist for most of her life. She spoke hauntingly of her "many regrets" about her time in Paris in the 1950s and 1960s—we had to use our imaginations. Through a series of unpredictable events in her latter years, she came to discard her deeply philosophical atheism in favor of a joyous encounter with Christianity. In a Christmas card she wrote to me shortly afterwards, she told how this old epicurean had come to treasure the biblical promises concerning the future—not the harps and halos, but the pledge that the Creator will renew all things, that he will provide us with "land." "I find this thought more and more inspiring," she wrote. "It gives me hope in the future. And I pray each night to be a modest helper toward that great goal of a New Creation."

This was a theme I was able to reflect on at her funeral, where I pointed out that the Bible's promise of restoration is the proper fulfillment of all of Marie's previous epicurean longings to experience the delights of creation. And it all begins with Abraham. God's promise to him assures him that the Creator intends to restore not only the *spiritual* and *social* dimensions of life but also the *physical* creation itself.

FROM ABRAHAM TO MOSES

Abraham's son Isaac had two sons, twins Jacob and Esau. Jacob, who was given the name "Israel" by God (which literally means he who struggles), in turn had twelve sons, the descendants of whom basically became the twelve tribes of Israel. Throughout the Genesis narrative, the promises to Abraham are reiterated to Isaac and Jacob. They become the bearers of the covenant—so much so that throughout the rest of the Bible, the Almighty is often introduced as "the God of Abraham, Isaac and Jacob."

One of Jacob's sons was named Joseph, of Technicolor dream coat fame. Joseph, the favorite son of his father, the object of hatred and envy on the part of his brothers, was sold into slavery by them and wound up in Egypt.

After years of suffering in Egypt, where he was a slave, wrongfully accused of a crime, thrown into prison, isolated, and lived in fear of death, Joseph was rescued by God and, through a series of divine set-ups, was promoted to be the pharaoh's right-hand man.

Meanwhile, Joseph's brothers, who were affected by a famine, came to Egypt to buy food, and they were reunited with Joseph, who welcomed them with one of the most magnanimous declarations in the Bible: "You intended to harm me, but God intended it for good to accomplish what is now being done, the saving of many lives. So then, don't be afraid. I will provide for you and your children" (Genesis 50:20–21a).

At the end of Genesis, there are seventy people who are the descendants of Abraham, which

Abraham to Moses (dates of early Israelite history are contested by scholars)

Timeline		Abraham	Isaac	Jacob (Joseph)
2100 BC	2000	1900	1800	1700

Israel's time in Egypt c. 1876 – 1445

is not bad for a single extended family, but it is not quite the great nation that was promised. Nor are they in the Promised Land. They are in Egypt.

As you turn over the page from Genesis to the book of Exodus, the growing Israelites find themselves under the tyranny of a new Egyptian pharaoh. We wonder how the threefold promise to Abraham—the restoration of the spiritual, social, and physical dimensions of existence—will ever get back on track. How will the goals of God's good world possibly be achieved?

Here we meet the great biblical figure of Moses. Moses' story is told largely in Exodus, the second book of the Bible. It is extraordinary and worth reading in full. Moses was chosen by God to lead the Israelites out of slavery in Egypt to the Promised Land.

In the Moses story we see some of the most extraordinary miracles—the burning bush, the parting of the Red Sea, manna from heaven, water from a rock—but, more than the spectacle, this story is remarkable for the way it reveals God's intense love for his people. He hears them when they pray to him out of suffering, and he acts to save them. The event of their rescue from Egypt is known as the Exodus, and it strongly foreshadows the even greater salvation that would occur in Jesus in the New Testament. Moses not only "saves" his people, but he gives them a new law, beginning with the famous Ten Commandments.

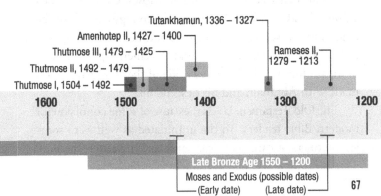

Tutankhamun, 1336 – 1327
Amenhotep II, 1427 – 1400
Thutmose III, 1479 – 1425
Thutmose II, 1492 – 1479
Thutmose I, 1504 – 1492
Rameses II, 1279 – 1213

| 1600 | 1500 | 1400 | 1300 | 1200 |

Late Bronze Age 1550 – 1200
Moses and Exodus (possible dates)
(Early date)   (Late date)

67

4

THE GOOD LIFE: MOSES AND HIS LAW

KEEP HIS DECREES AND COMMANDS, WHICH I AM GIVING YOU TODAY, SO THAT IT MAY GO WELL WITH YOU AND YOUR CHILDREN AFTER YOU AND THAT YOU MAY LIVE LONG IN THE LAND THE LORD YOUR GOD GIVES YOU FOR ALL TIME. (DEUTERONOMY 4:40)

After several hundred years as a slave-nation in Egypt, God saved the descendants of Abraham, the Israelites, by bringing them out of the great superpower that Egyptologists call the "New Kingdom" (16th – 11th centuries BC). Through their leader and deliverer, Moses, God gave Israel *a law*, a kind of national constitution to regulate life in the land God was soon to give them. It outlines Israel's response to God's great act of salvation and the emerging fulfillment of his promises. It is the *human* side of the "covenant" God made with Abraham and his descendants.

The Old Testament law is the cause of some confusion for modern Bible readers. To the uninitiated as well as to some long-termers, it can seem dense and baffling and sometimes offensive. Christians have even been known, perhaps out of a desire to appease or out of ignorance, to create a stark division between the Old Testament law and the New Testament story, as if they have little to do with one another, almost as though the Old Testament is the "problem" of which the New Testament is the "solution." But there is profound continuity between Old and New Testaments, and as long as we follow those connections, the law given to Moses is a great pointer to the ministry of Jesus and a source of wisdom for life.

THE PREMISE OF THE LAW

Both New and Old Testament covenants are predicated on the simple notion that grace always *precedes* obedience, as we saw with Abraham, the first Israelite. Before God gives any laws to the descendants of Abraham, there is a long description of the salvation of Israel from Egypt:

> Then Moses went up to God, and the LORD called to him from the mountain and said, "This is what you are to say to the descendants of Jacob and what you are to tell the people of Israel: 'You yourselves have seen what I did to Egypt, and how I carried you on eagles' wings and brought you to myself. Now if you obey me fully and keep my covenant, then out of all nations you will be my treasured possession. Although the whole earth is mine, you will be for me a kingdom of priests and a holy nation. These are the words you are to speak to the Israelites.' " (Exodus 19:3–6)

Again, in the next chapter of Exodus, immediately before we hear the first laws, the famous Ten Commandments, we read, "I am the LORD your God, who brought you out of Egypt, out of the land of slavery" (Exodus 20:2). We need to pause here and consider the significance of this deliverance from Egypt.

It is hard to overstate the importance of the rescue from Egypt, the "exodus," in Israel's consciousness. The Israelites had arrived in the land of the pharaohs in a time of peace. As the years rolled on, however, things changed dramatically. Israel grew to become a substantial minority in Egypt, and as so often happens after periods of immigration, the host nation turned on the newcomers. Pharaoh turned them into a slave nation, working under impossible conditions to satisfy Egyptian expansion programs: "So they [the Egyptians] put slave masters over them to oppress them with forced labor, and they built Pithom and Rameses as store cities for Pharaoh. But the more they were oppressed, the more they multiplied and spread; so the Egyptians came to dread the Israelites and worked them ruthlessly" (Exodus 1:11 – 13). Israel cried out to the God who had made promises to Abraham, and God intervened, bringing terrible judgment on Egypt and leading the Israelites out.

I frequently hear people say there is no evidence for the biblical story of an exodus from Egypt. Where is the archaeology? Why didn't the Egyptians record it? The question, of course, is a slightly loaded one. It assumes that the biblical record itself is not evidence. It surely must be considered as evidence, just as testimony in a court of law is "evidence," even when it can't be corroborated by other witnesses. It is right to say there is no Egyptian evidence of a massive escape of a slave nation from their midst: no hieroglyphs recording such a shameful loss, no archaeological remains of deluged chariots, and no physical indication of a huge camp of Israelites moving north toward Canaan.

This argument would be powerfully significant if we had tons of Egyptian evidence for other events from this period. But we don't. It is one of the frustrating aspects of ancient history, especially from this period, that scholars have to piece together their picture of events from tiny fragments of entirely unrepresentative data. Which documents, inscriptions, and archaeological items survive and which don't is entirely hit-and-miss and woefully incomplete. We don't have even 1 percent of the records of the New Kingdom. And with more than 99 percent of the evidence missing, who can say for sure what did *not* happen?

We can be confident there were Semitic peoples (like the Israelites) enslaved in large numbers in Egypt during the New Kingdom period. We also know—from one surviving Egyptian inscription known as the Merneptah Stele—that a people group called "Israel" was living in Canaan by 1210 BC. This is at least consistent with the biblical timeline, which has the exodus occurring somewhere between 1450 and 1250 BC and Israel's occupation of the land by 1200 BC at the latest. Beyond that, skeptics and believers have to fall back on their underlying convictions and preferences to form opinions about the exodus.

BOOK NOTES

When asked about Old Testament history, I always recommend K. A. Kitchen's *On the Reliability of the Old Testament* (Eerdmans, 2006). Professor Kitchen is not a theologian but an Egyptologist from the University of Liverpool, who has turned his considerable expertise to important questions about the origins of Israel, especially the exodus from Egypt. Despite the title—which I doubt Kitchen came up with—this is not a work of Christian "apologetics," but it does systematically demolish the arguments of many Old Testaments critics who are "factually disadvantaged or who do not do their Near Eastern homework," as William W. Hallo, professor of Assyriology and Babylonian literature at Yale University, says on the back cover of Kitchen's book.

On the night of the exodus itself, the Israelites were instructed to kill and eat a lamb and to place some of its blood on their doorposts. When God came in judgment on Egypt later that evening, he observed the sign of blood and passed over those Jewish households. This is the famous Passover, even today one of the most sacred festivals in the Jewish calendar, which commemorates God's pledge to rescue his people. Christians, under the influence of Jesus' own teaching, would later think of his death and the blood shed on the cross as the ultimate "Passover" for the salvation of the world. But that is to get way ahead of ourselves.

My point for now is that this extraordinary event of redemption is the *premise* of the laws God gave to Israel through Moses. God does not say, "If you will obey me,

I will save you." He speaks these laws to the already saved people of Israel. Grace remains the premise of the law. God reminds the Israelites that they are already loved, already saved, already his people. It is because of this reality—not as the path to achieving it—that Israel is to obey God. The structure is exactly the same as the structure of Abraham's call, mentioned earlier: grace first, obedience second; rescue before a life of righteousness. It is, as I have said, a golden thread throughout the Bible.

I will never forget meeting a young man after a lecture I gave at his school in New South Wales. Intrigued by my mentions of "God" (yes, we can say that word in Australian schools), he showed me a notebook in which he had drawn up accounting columns. Across the top of the page were the days of the week. Down the left-hand column he had listed a number of ethical virtues—patience, kindness, compassion, and the like. For each virtue across the days of the week, he had given himself a score out of ten, for pages and pages. He wanted to know if this was an effective way to work out whether God thought favorably toward him. I didn't know whether to laugh or cry. Instead, I explained to him the biblical connection between virtue and favor, between our performance and God's mercy. I had the great pleasure of watching him walk over to the school rubbish bin and throw his notebook away with great gusto.

Mercy isn't just the *first premise* of the Old Testament law; it is also the *ongoing assumption* of the law. A huge proportion of the laws in the Old Testament are about how to conduct sacrifices for atonement. These are not appendices to the law. Nor are they a kind of "escape clause," after hearing about how onerous the law is. The mercy laws are built into the fabric of the law, as if to say that God expects his people to sin, and he expects his people to turn back to him, and he expects his people to know that he will forgive them.

A classic example of this principle of forgiveness-at-the-heart-of-law is in the book of Leviticus, the third book of the Bible. Here, many of Israel's laws are found. Some feel it is one of the driest parts of the Old Testament. I'm not so sure. Of course, no legal text—let alone national legislation—is exactly light reading, but mercy fills this book in beautiful ways. Leviticus 15 and 17 contain typical instructions about how the ancient Jews were to conduct their day-to-day lives. Sandwiched between these sections, as part-and-parcel of the Old Testament law, is Leviticus 16, a description of Yom Kippur, the great Day of Atonement, a key Jewish festival in which the sins of all the people were forgiven:

> When Aaron has finished making atonement for the Most Holy Place, the tent of meeting and the altar, he shall bring forward the live goat. He is to lay both hands on the head of the live goat and confess over it all the wickedness and rebellion of the Israelites—all their sins—and put them on the goat's head. He shall send the goat away into the wilderness in the care of someone appointed for the task. The goat will carry on itself all their sins to a remote place; and the man shall release it in the wilderness....
>
> This is to be a lasting ordinance for you: On the tenth day of the seventh month you must deny yourselves and not do any work—whether native-born or a foreigner residing among you—because on this day atonement will be made for you, to cleanse you. Then, before the LORD, you will be clean from all your sins. (Leviticus 16:20–30)

Sacrifice was not an adjunct failure clause. It is central to Old Testament law. It was a reminder not only that Israel would fail to obey God perfectly but also that God stood ready to pardon all who humbly looked to him for mercy. Although all of this occurs centuries before Jesus, it was also the perfect pointer to all that Jesus would bring. He was a new lawgiver, a kind of Moses figure, and he would give his own life as the ultimate Day of Atonement sacrifice for all who look to God for mercy.

THE SHAPE OF THE LAW

The *shape* of the Old Testament law is essentially the same as that of the New Testament expectations about life. It is vertical and horizontal, partly about love for God and partly about love for neighbor. The Ten Commandments, which introduce all of Israel's laws, are four commandments about what one does for God, followed by six commandments about the treatment of others:

I am the LORD your God, who brought you out of Egypt, out of the land of slavery [there's that emphasis on prior grace again].

1. You shall have no other gods before me.
2. You shall not make for yourself an image in the form of anything in heaven above or on the earth beneath or in the waters below....
3. You shall not misuse the name of the LORD your God, for the LORD will not hold anyone guiltless who misuses his name.

4. Observe the Sabbath day by keeping it holy, as the LORD your God has commanded you. Six days you shall labor and do all your work, but the seventh day is a sabbath to the LORD your God....

5. Honor your father and your mother, as the LORD your God has commanded you, so that you may live long and that it may go well with you in the land the LORD your God is giving you.

6. You shall not murder.

7. You shall not commit adultery.

8. You shall not steal.

9. You shall not give false testimony against your neighbor.

10. You shall not covet your neighbor's wife. You shall not set your desire on your neighbor's house or land, his male or female servant, his ox or donkey, or anything that belongs to your neighbor. (Deuteronomy 5:6–21)

The structure of the law, from these Ten Commandments right through the rest of the Jewish law, is about *love for God* and *love for neighbor*. There are many more laws in the Old Testament than these ten, of course, and some of them sound strange to modern ears, but they all conform to this general shape. They are either about the regard we must show to our Maker or the honor we are to show other creatures.

This pattern does not essentially change in the New Testament. When Jesus was asked twelve hundred or so years after Moses, "Which is the greatest commandment in the Law?" he disputed the premise of the question. He was asked to give the *single* greatest commandment, but Jesus replied there were *two*: "Love the Lord your God with all your heart and with all your soul and with all your mind. This is the first and greatest commandment. And the second is like it: Love your neighbor as yourself. All the Law and the Prophets hang on these two commandments" (Matthew 22:37–40). To separate love of God from love of neighbor, or vice versa, is to miss the point of God's will.

The person who is God-fearing and God-praising, a regular church-going, Bible-reading evangelist and yet who is harsh and unloving toward the people in her life, has absolutely failed to uphold God's law. The flipside is also true. The humanist or social reformer, who is full of goodwill toward fellow humans but is cold and unthankful toward the God who gives life and breath to all things, has also failed the Almighty. Both the religious hypocrite and the moral atheist commit equal and opposite errors — they separate the love of God from the love of fellow humans, and, according to the Old Testament law and Jesus Christ, we simply cannot do this.

A CHARTER OF FREEDOM

The Old Testament constantly describes its laws as "life," "joy," "blessing," and true "freedom." This will puzzle a modern reader, who is used to thinking of freedom as the power to choose any course of action. Surely "thou-shalt-not," a phrase repeated endlessly in the Ten Commandments, is the epitome of restriction and authoritarianism. Well, no! This confuses sentence grammar with practical reality. Of course the Ten Commandments are stated negatively — for the simple reason that only a few things really are forbidden and pretty much everything else is there to be enjoyed. Would we really want positive commands—lists of what we are allowed to do? If you're at the top of a snow-covered mountain, do you want to be told the 450 different ways you may ski down, or would you prefer to be told the few rough patches to avoid so that the rest of the hill is yours? No one puts it better than the early twentieth-century British intellectual G. K. Chesterton:

> This is particularly plain in the fuss about "negative morality," or what may be described as the campaign against the Ten Commandments. The truth is, of course, that the curtness of the Commandments is an evidence, not of the gloom and narrowness of a religion, but, on the contrary, of its liberality and humanity. It is shorter to state the things forbidden than the things permitted, precisely because most things are permitted and only a few things are forbidden. An optimist who insisted on a purely positive morality would have to begin (supposing he knew where to begin) by telling a man that he might pick dandelions on a common, and go on for months before he came to the fact that he might throw pebbles into the sea; and then resume his untiring efforts by issuing a general permission to sneeze, to make snowballs, to blow bubbles, to play marbles, to make toy aeroplanes, to travel on Tooting trams, and everything else he could think of, without ever coming to an end. In comparison with this positive morality, the Ten Commandments rather shine in that brevity which is the soul of wit. It is better to tell a man not to steal than to try to tell him the thousand things that he can enjoy without stealing; especially as

he can generally be pretty well trusted to enjoy them.
(*The Complete Works of G K Chesterton* [Ignatius Press,
1989], 32:18)

"Freedom" today is often defined as the power to choose
any course of action. "Live and let live" is the only rule.
Many talk like this, but it can't be right. Freedom cannot
be the capacity to do whatever we choose. Some choices are
destructive and enslaving, to ourselves and to others. Speak
to an alcoholic, a workaholic, the young man addicted to
pornography, the tragic adulterer, the friendless millionaire.
Some "free" choices are enslaving.

"Freedom" is surely better defined as the ability to become
what I am made for. As contemporary philosopher and theologian David Bentley Hart writes, "We are free not merely
because we can choose, but only when we have chosen well.
For to choose poorly, through folly or malice, in a way that
thwarts our nature and distorts our proper form, is to enslave
ourselves to the transitory, the irrational, the purposeless"
(*Atheist Delusions* [Yale University Press, 2009], 25).

Christians have always said that living God's way puts us
in harmony with God's world and with his purposes for our
lives. God's ways "work" in the way that a manufacturer's
instructions work or the advice of an expert works. In the
Old Testament, this promise held the form of blessing and
long life in the land God had given Israel: "Keep his decrees
and commands, which I am giving you today, so that it may
go well with you and your children after you and that you
may live long in the land the LORD your God gives you for
all time" (Deuteronomy 4:40).

Obviously, things are different in the New Testament,

for there is no promised land to live in, and the same blessings are not pronounced on all our material endeavors—contrary to the assurances of the contemporary prosperity preachers. Nevertheless, the New Testament does say that following God's ways, what is called "godliness," has more than simply "eternal" benefits. The apostle Paul reminds his apprentice Timothy, "For physical training is of some value, but godliness has value for all things, holding promise for both the present life and the life to come" (1 Timothy 4:8). Obedience to God is not a formula for health, wealth, and happiness; often it brings suffering and pain. But the benefits of living God's way in God's world are real, as believers will usually testify.

To offer an analogy: I recently crossed a threshold in my skiing. For years I have been too proud to take lessons, content to carve up the slopes in my own effective but not exactly pretty style. In convincing my son to take a lesson last season, I somehow convinced myself it was my time, too. The lesson was a little frustrating at first. The technical way in which the instructor broke down the turn felt onerous—he had me concentrating on timing, edging, weight distribution on each foot, and so on, all at the same time. About halfway through the lesson something clicked. Turns began to take care of themselves. I was no longer fighting the boots, the skis, or the snow. I was free. It turns out the instructor's directives were not "restrictions," but paths to liberty in my favorite pastime.

Surfers say the same thing: there's a moment when you do things just right and you become free on the wave. Singers echo the sentiment—only when you're in time and in tune are you free. The analogies could be multiplied. The point is the same. God's ways, embodied in his commandments to love him and those around us, are what we're made for, and when we follow them, we are *free* in the true sense.

THE CHARGE OF INCONSISTENCY

For all the *continuity* between the Old and New Testaments, it is equally clear that there are significant *discontinuities*, and it is here that numerous modern misunderstandings about the place of the law of Moses emerge. Indeed, contemporary skeptics frequently have a field day pointing out the differences between Moses and Jesus, between the Old and New Testaments. This is meant to create a problem for Christian faith, exposing it as a pick-and-choose religion, inconsistently affirming some bits of the Old Testament, while arbitrarily avoiding others.

No one has leveled this charge of inconsistency against Christians better than Aaron Sorkin, creator of the superb television series *The West Wing*. In an episode from season 2, Sorkin has President Jed Bartlet powerfully confront a Christian talk show host, Dr. Jenna Jacobs, at a White House event. Bartlet mocks Jacobs' on-air statements about homosexuality as "an abomination." She tries to defend herself by pointing that it is the Bible—a statement from the Old Testament book of Leviticus—that uses the word "abomination" of same sex activity. This is all the biblically literate, and inordinately articulate, President needs to launch into a tirade against the inconsistency of Jacobs.

I wanted to ask you a couple of questions while I had you here. I'm interested in selling my youngest daughter into slavery as sanctioned in Exodus 21:7. She's a Georgetown sophomore, speaks fluent Italian, always cleared the table when it was her turn. What would a good price for her be? While thinking about that, can I ask another? My chief of staff Leo McGarry insists on working on the Sabbath. Exodus 35:2 clearly says he should be put to death. Am I morally obligated to kill him myself, or is it okay to call the police? Here's one that's really important, because we've got a lot of sports fans in this town and touching the skin of a dead pig makes one unclean (Leviticus 11:7). If they promise to wear gloves, can the Washington Redskins still play football? Can Notre Dame? Can West Point? Does the whole town really have to be together to stone my brother John for planting different crops side by side? Can I burn my mother in a small family gathering for wearing garments made from two different threads? Think about those questions, would you! (*The West Wing*: The Midterms [#2.3], 2000)

Dr. Jenna Jacobs responds with crushed silenced, and the audience (both in the scene and at home watching the episode) cringes. It is an extraordinary piece of television and has gone viral on YouTube.

Variations of this reasoning have now entered into our culture as the knockdown argument against Christians using the Bible as a source of ethics. If you take one thing from the Old Testament and not another, you are charged with cherry-picking and being inconsistent, and since most of the Old Testament laws seem irrelevant or unfair for life today, you can dismiss the Bible and the Christians who follow it.

The problem with this line of thinking is that it ignores how Christians have read the Old Testament law from the very beginning. It is not the case that modern-day Christians pick and choose the bits of the Bible they like based on cultural climate or a liking for pork (something forbidden in Jewish law). Christians have always understood the Old Testament law as *fulfilled* by Jesus.

Let me offer an imperfect but helpful analogy. When light passes through a prism, it *refracts*. The different wavelengths break into the spectrum of colors (as perceived by the human eye), as in the case of a rainbow. Imagine the laws of Moses as a light passing through the prism of Jesus' life, teaching, death, and resurrection. The light "refracts." It comes out the other side in its full spectrum. Some Old Testament laws are refracted only a little (such as the need to care for the poor); others are refracted beyond recognition (as in the case of food laws and death penalties); still others are intensified ("love your neighbor" in the teaching of Moses becomes "love your enemy" in the teaching of Jesus). It probably sounds like cherry-picking when you first contemplate this idea, but as you read the New Testament more and more, and read the Old Testament in light of the New, it becomes easier and easier to spot all the ways the coming of Jesus has refracted the law of Israel.

The Old Testament itself expected and looked forward to this "refraction" in what it called the "new covenant." There was an understanding in the Old Testament that there would one day be a new agreement (which is what "covenant" means) between God and humanity, and this would transform the laws.

Moses himself said that God would provide another guide: "The LORD your God will raise up for you *a prophet like me* from among you, from your fellow Israelites. You must listen to him" (Deuteronomy 18:15, italics added). Curiously, the closing lines of this same Old Testament book make clear that, long after Moses, Israel was still waiting for the "prophet like Moses": "Since then, no prophet has risen in Israel like Moses" (Deuteronomy 34:10). Old Testament scholars Tremper Longman III and Raymond Dillard say this simple syllogism influenced Jewish interpreters:

1. God will raise up a prophet like Moses (chap. 18).
2. There has not been a prophet like Moses (chap. 34).

Therefore, we must keep looking for such a prophet (*An Introduction to the Old Testament* [2nd edition; Zondervan, 2006], 118).

Needless to say, centuries later the writers of the New Testament would say that Jesus is in fact the "prophet like Moses" that Israel was waiting for (Acts 3:19–22).

More to the point, the Old Testament prophet Jeremiah (six hundred years after Moses and six hundred years before Jesus) wrote of a new agreement/covenant that would eclipse the former one:

> "The days are coming," declares the LORD,
>   "when I will make a new covenant
> with the people of Israel
>   and with the people of Judah.
> It will not be like the covenant
>   I made with their ancestors
> when I took them by the hand

> to lead them out of Egypt,
> because they broke my covenant,
>> though I was a husband to them,"
>>> declares the LORD.
> "This is the covenant I will make with the people of
>> Israel
>> after that time," declares the LORD.
> "I will put my law in their minds
>> and write it on their hearts.
> I will be their God,
>> and they will be my people.
> No longer will they teach their neighbor,
>> or say to one another, 'Know the LORD,'
> because they will all know me,
>> from the least of them to the greatest,"
>>> declares the LORD.
> "For I will forgive their wickedness
>> and will remember their sins no more."
>>> (Jeremiah 31:31–34)

According to the New Testament centuries later, this new covenant came into effect through Jesus Christ. It is still the fulfillment of the covenant with Abraham, but its fresh outlook and demands mean that it is, in a real sense, "new." As a result, when Christians read the Old Testament, they interpret it *through Jesus*. The light of Old Testament law is refracted through the prism of the Christ-event.

Christians have always read the Old Testament this way. This is not some fancy footwork designed by modern Christian apologists to get out of the charge of inconsistency leveled at them by the likes of President Jed Bartlet. It is the way Jesus taught his followers to approach the Old

Testament. It is how the Old Testament itself said that it would one day be read.

BOOK NOTES

For those who want to explore much more deeply the way the New Testament handles the laws of the Old Testament, there is no more important recent book than the volume by Brian Rosner, *Paul and the Law: Keeping the Commandments of God* (InterVarsity Press, 2013). The book focuses on the letters of the apostle Paul, who talked about the law more than any other New Testament author. It is more a piece of (accessible) scholarship than a popular introduction, but it is a wonderfully clarifying treatment of an often highly confusing subject.

This is not to say we won't stumble across parts of Old Testament law that we find confusing or even distasteful, but critics have to pay Christians the respect of listening to how they read their own documents. The continuity between the Old and New Testaments is real—the shape and premise are the same. The discontinuity emerges not from some patch-up job of a pick-and-choose religion. The Old Testament itself spoke of its own inbuilt redundancy and of the future arrival of a new Moses and a new covenant. The Old Testament remains God's Word, but it must be read taking into account Jesus' life, teaching, death, and resurrection—the "prism" showing God's light in the full spectrum of color.

FROM MOSES TO THE END OF JOSHUA

After God gives the laws to Moses, the Israelites make a forty-year journey through the wilderness (it should have taken a couple of weeks but that's another story!) before arriving at the edge of the Promised Land, where Moses reiterates the laws, in the book called Deuteronomy or "second law," and tells the people to get their hearts (and weapons) ready to take the land from the Canaanites.

The bloody battles that follow are recorded in the book of Joshua, named after Israel's military commander who succeeded Moses as leader of God's people.

From Moses to End of Joshua

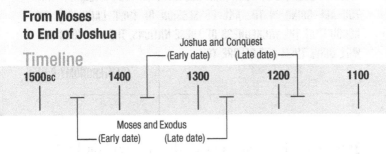

Timeline

Joshua and Conquest
— (Early date)   (Late date) —

| 1500BC | 1400 | 1300 | 1200 | 1100 |

Moses and Exodus
— (Early date)   (Late date) —

5

JUSTICE FOR ALL: THE VIOLENCE OF JOSHUA AND THE LOVE OF GOD

IT IS NOT BECAUSE OF YOUR RIGHTEOUSNESS OR YOUR INTEGRITY THAT YOU ARE GOING IN TO TAKE POSSESSION OF THEIR LAND; BUT ON ACCOUNT OF THE WICKEDNESS OF THESE NATIONS, THE Lᴏʀᴅ YOUR GOD WILL DRIVE THEM OUT BEFORE YOU.

(DEUTERONOMY 9:5)

It is hard to know how to feel when you read the book of Joshua. On the one hand, this is a book about the fulfillment of the third dimension of the promise to Abraham: to receive a land. Israel has been called, loved, and rescued from Egypt by God: the *spiritual* dimension. The people have been constituted as a nation with their own divine constitution, the law: the *social* dimension. A generation after the exodus, they are about to enter Canaan and receive the Promised Land: the *physical* dimension. All of God's pledges are coming to pass.

But it is also a dreadful moment, especially to modern ears, because the conquering of land of Canaan meant the dispossession of the Canaanites. In some ways, the book of Joshua seems to stand for everything many dislike about the Old Testament—xenophobia, ethnic cleansing, and violence in the name of God. It is not immediately obvious how we are to square any of this with the teaching and life of Jesus.

In his bestselling book *The God Delusion,* Richard Dawkins articulates well his horror at what he reads in Joshua: "The ethnic cleansing begun in the time of Moses is brought to bloody fruition in the book of Joshua, a text remarkable for the bloodthirsty massacres it records and the xenophobic relish with which it does so" (Richard Dawkins, *The God Delusion* [Bantam Press, 2006], 247). Elsewhere he writes, "The god of the Old Testament has got to be the most unpleasant character in all fiction. Jealous and proud of it, petty, vindictive, unjust, unforgiving, racist. An ethnic cleanser urging his people on to acts of genocide" (*The God Delusion*, 31).

I have a good deal of respect for Richard Dawkins. And he is right that there are some terribly violent bits in the book of Joshua. I want to suggest, however, that a careful reading of the book of Joshua shows that what is going on in these pages has nothing to do with ethnic cleansing. The stories recounted do contain violence, and that is difficult, but it is not xenophobic violence. In fact, the book makes this plain from its opening narratives.

GOD ON OUR SIDE?

In the second chapter of Joshua, there is a strange story of a prostitute named Rahab who lives in the Canaanite city of

Jericho. Despite the fact that she is a Canaanite, she shelters Israelite spies because she believes in the Israelite God. Consequently, she and her family are offered salvation; not only are they spared in the coming battle between the Israelites and her countrymen, but she is accorded great honor in Israel's history and even gets a mention centuries later in the genealogy of Jesus. And in the New Testament book of James she is presented as a model of faith.

Rahab is an odd character to include in the book of Joshua, which is essentially a military account, especially as the opening narrative. Why has the ancient author begun this way? It seems obvious that the narrator is trying to state up-front that God wishes to save the Canaanites (even ones with dubious professions). The violence that will be brought against Canaan is real, but it is not about racial or religious hatred. As we will see, it is entirely about something else.

The next major story in the book of Joshua—immediately before the first battle scene—has Israel's commander standing on the edge of Jericho ready for the fight. An angelic figure suddenly appears. Readers' expectations are raised. Here is where we would expect God to confirm his approval of the Israelites and hatred of the Canaanites. After all, that is what "holy war" is all about, we imagine. Not in the Bible! This divine messenger has a striking message to deliver:

> Now when Joshua was near Jericho, he looked up and saw a man standing in front of him with a drawn sword in his hand. Joshua went up to him and asked "Are you for us or for our enemies?"
>
> "Neither," he replied. "But as commander of the army of the LORD I have now come." (Joshua 5:13–14)

The scene is counterintuitive in an ancient context. When asked which nation the angel was there to support, he replies, "Neither." God seems to be making it plain that what is about to happen has nothing to do with *ethnicity*. It would be inappropriate to accept the brute fact of the military stories in Joshua but overlook these key narrative markers about *how to read* the stories. If the so called "new atheism" had a few more literati instead of a preponderance of physical scientists, it might be a different kind of movement. It certainly would pause more often to understand what the Bible is saying and how it is saying it instead of simply mining the text for stories to complain about.

WAR AS JUDGMENT

What was the conquest of Canaan all about if not ethnic cleansing? The answer comes from no higher source than Moses, who in his speeches on the edge of the Promised Land, months before the battles began, made clear that God had no intention of playing favorites:

> After the LORD your God has driven [the Canaanites] out before you, do not say to yourself, "The LORD has brought me here to take possession of this land because of my righteousness." No, it is on account of the wickedness of these nations that the LORD is going to drive them out before you. It is not because of your righteousness or your integrity that you are going in to take possession of their land; but on account of the wickedness of these nations, the LORD your God will drive them out before you.... Understand, then, that it is not because of your

righteousness that the LORD your God is giving you this
good land to possess, for you are a stiff-necked people.
(Deuteronomy 9:4–6)

In Hebrew storytelling, if you want to underline a point,
you say it over and over. The point Moses is making with
such repetitive force is that God is not driving out the
Canaanites because they are Canaanites, but rather because
they are wicked—and their wickedness has nothing to do
with their being Canaanites (as the story of Rahab shows).
This is not God playing favorites. It has nothing to do with
xenophobia. God is bringing judgment on a people whose
wickedness has reached a climax. Canaan was a land of
rapacious greed and terrible oppression, a land that practiced
ritual prostitution and child sacrifice (to the god Molech),
both profound acts of demeaning those made in God's
image. It was a truly terrible place.

Of course, we are at liberty not to believe the biblical
evaluation of Canaan, but then there would be little basis
for critiquing these conquests in the first place. For perhaps the war against Canaan didn't happen either. Problem
solved. My point, of course, is that a double standard is in
play if we accept the scriptural account of a war against
Canaan and then reject the Scriptural *grounds* for that war.
As I will explain below, Israel had little reason to invent a
pretext for war.

To be clear, the point is not that the Canaanites were
sinful unbelievers and the Israelites righteous believers. The
passage just quoted makes plain that Israel itself was far
from righteous. Indeed, they were "a stiff-necked people,"
a euphemism for stubbornly disobedient. The Israelite

armies—which, keep in mind, were tiny and powerless compared to those of the Canaanites—were not a "holy" and "deserving" instrument of the divine will; they were themselves an unworthy tool in the righteous hands of God. The Bible's "holy war" language is nothing like the "holy war" language of other cultures—ancient and modern—which tends to lay stress on "goodies" and "baddies." There are only "baddies" in this narrative. It is just that one group had reached a *crescendo* of evil that the Almighty would no longer bear.

It is worth noting in passing that it would be wrong to imagine that any of this was an invention of the ancient biblical authors to make them seem humble and self-effacing in the midst of a patently repugnant act of brutality. That would be an entirely anachronistic reading, as if the authors of Joshua and Deuteronomy were conscious of contemporary sensitivities about religious and racial violence. No. Ancient cultures required no such justification. They had no problem with the idea of swooping in and taking someone else's land. Indeed, that is what made nations great in antiquity. In the second millennium BC one did not need a "pretext," such as "Canaan is really, really wicked," to justify military action. One simply acted and gloried in the victory (or suffered loss). Yet here it is in Israel's own official history—a powerful statement that none of the players is righteous (neither the victors nor the vanquished) and that God is using Israel merely as an instrument to exact his judgment.

I have often been asked why God did not step in and condemn the Nazis, why God did not step in and condemn the death squads that walked over Tasmania killing Aborigines, why God did not step in and condemn Pol Pot as he slaughtered two million of his eight million countrymen. These are questions we wrestle with. We want God to act. The book of Joshua says there was a moment in history—a brief, limited moment—when God did just that, when he meted out justice through the Israelites to a nation whose wickedness had surpassed what the Creator was willing to tolerate.

If God condemned every wicked nation, we would lose heart (and who would be left to discuss the problem?). If he never displayed his judgment in verifiable history, we might doubt that he really is the God of justice that the Bible claims. We might conclude that promises of future judgment were just idle threats of a moralistic culture. But God gave a limited, concrete, and entirely just "historical marker" that would echo through the ages as a sign of the reality of his judgment. God did to the Canaanites what we wish he'd done on the "killing fields" or at Auschwitz. He did it *once* to show he is serious—*only* once so we might know his mercy.

JUDGE JESUS

One of the reasons people shrink from the idea of God's judgment is that the church has talked about it so badly. You hear stories of so-called Christians who preach that a certain group of people, or people who have committed a certain sin, will burn in hell forever, and they say this with such relish that you can almost imagine them gleefully warming their hands over hell's fires as they watch the "wicked" suffer.

I met Judy some years ago, who told me that she had

heard a sermon thirty-five years ago in which the preacher spoke of God's judgment with a smile. She said, "I walked out of church and decided never, ever to go back." I had the privilege of seeing her rediscover Christian faith before she died, and then of conducting her funeral. But you can see why she was so turned off by the incident. Not only is it inhumane to delight in the suffering of others; it is simply not how the Bible speaks about judgment. Jesus, hanging on the cross, prays for those who have nailed him there: "Father, forgive them, for they do not know what they are doing" (Luke 23:34). And at one point Jesus reflects on the judgment that will come on Israel and cries out: "Jerusalem, Jerusalem ... how often I have longed to gather your children together, as a hen gathers her chicks under her wings, and you were not willing" (Luke 13:34). The situation is no different in the Old Testament. In the book of Ezekiel, God says, "I take no pleasure in the death of anyone" (Ezekiel 18:32).

If we are honest with ourselves, however, there is probably another reason we recoil from the notion of divine judgment: we do not want to be judged. We object to being under moral scrutiny, and so we choose to caricature talk of judgment as the old "fire-and-brimstone religion" that is out of place in a today's tolerant world. The Old Testament portrays a cranky, judgmental God, we say, but Jesus is all about love and peace. He would never say a harsh word to anyone. So our preferences assure us.

In reality, the theme of God as judge, as exemplified in book of Joshua, does not disappear in the New Testament. It is transposed, for sure—or "refracted"—but some of the most terrifying descriptions of future judgment are actually found in the New Testament. And it's Jesus who is the judge. Revelation, the final book of the Bible, contains the following description of Jesus:

> I saw heaven standing open and there before me was a white horse, whose rider is called Faithful and True. With justice he judges and wages war. His eyes are like blazing fire, and on his head are many crowns. He has a name written on him that no one knows but he himself. He is dressed in a robe dipped in blood, and his name is the Word of God. The armies of heaven were following him, riding on white horses and dressed in fine linen, white and clean. Coming out of his mouth is a sharp sword with which to strike down the nations. "He will rule them with an iron scepter." He treads the winepress of the fury of the wrath of God Almighty. (Revelation 19:11 – 15)

This is not a picture of Jesus many like to ponder. We prefer the idea of Jesus meek and mild, who tells people to turn the other cheek, preaches peace, and welcomes little children. But we must not fashion Jesus in our own image. The New Testament makes clear (repeatedly) that the judgment of Canaan was a limited historical sign of what will occur on a global scale when Jesus judges the world.

And yet, mercy always remains on offer. Just as the book of Joshua begins with the story of Rahab, so the book of Revelation uses literary cues, right in the middle of its judgment scenes, to assure readers that God wishes to pardon those who deserve his punishment. The victorious judge here in Revelation 19 is said to be "dressed in a robe dipped in blood." In the symbolic language of Revelation, which frequently refers to Jesus' blood, this can only be a reference to Jesus' death on the cross for the sins of the world. Even as he threatens justice, he holds out forgiveness.

INCOMPARABLE LOVE, INESCAPABLE JUDGMENT

However it might irk us, the Bible is unembarrassed in saying that the God of incomparable love is also the God of inescapable judgment. In fact, love and judgment often go together. It is precisely because God loves those who, for example, have experienced injustice and evil that he will bring his justice to bear on the perpetrators of evil. It is precisely Jesus' love for the poor, the exploited, the enslaved, the raped, the abused, and the murdered that prompts him to judge the perpetrators—and those who complacently allow such evil to continue.

Theologian Miroslav Volf was born in the former Yugoslavia. He saw his native country devastated by war and harsh rule, and he himself was suspected of being too closely tied to the West and underwent a series of horrific interrogations. He writes that when you see real suffering, it changes your perspective on the judgment of God. His larger argument concerns the crucial importance of nonviolence and reconciliation, which, he insists, requires a healthy belief in God's final "violence" or "judgment":

> One could object that it is not worthy of God to wield the sword. Is God not love, long-suffering and all-powerful love? [However] … in a world of violence it would not be worthy of God not to wield the sword; if God were not angry at injustice and deception and did not make the final end to violence God would not be worthy of our worship.…

My thesis that the practice of nonviolence requires a belief in divine vengeance will be unpopular. To the person who is inclined to dismiss it, I suggest imagining that you are delivering a lecture in a war zone. Among your listeners are people whose cities and villages have been first plundered, then burned and leveled to the ground, whose daughters and sisters have been raped, whose fathers and brothers have had their throats slit. The topic of the lecture: a Christian attitude toward violence. The thesis: we should not retaliate since God is perfect noncoercive love. Soon you would discover that it takes the quiet of a suburban home for the birth of the thesis that human nonviolence corresponds to God's refusal to judge. In a scorched land, soaked in the blood of the innocent, it will invariably die. (Miroslav Volf, *Exclusion and Embrace* [Abingdon, 1996], 303–4).

While the biblical warnings of divine judgment will continue to draw scorn from some, believers find comfort in the thought that these warnings — as with the judgment itself — arise from divine love.

A chilling reminder of the importance of such warnings comes from the awful 2011 tsunami that devastated the low-lying regions of the east coast of Japan. The waves, up to forty meters, traveled ten kilometers inland, leaving 20,000 people dead. Until recently, I never knew that the hills along the coast of Japan are dotted with hundreds of historical stone markers, some six hundred years old. These were ancient warnings not to build below certain lines on account of the remembered tsunamis. In the town of Aneyoshi one reads: "High dwellings are the peace and harmony of our descendants. Remember the calamity of the great tsunamis. Do not build any homes below this point." One in Kesennuma states: "Always be prepared for unexpected tsunamis. Choose life over your possessions and valuables." (See, further, Jay Alabaster, "Tsunami-Hit Towns Forgot Warnings from Ancestors," Associated Press, April 6, 2011).

My point here is not to draw any link between tsunamis and God's judgment—I hope that much is clear! It is to stress the importance of historical markers, of heeding the warnings of the past. According to the biblical narrative, the conquest of Canaan stands as a historical marker warning us that God's judgment is not a theological abstraction. We are meant to read the warning and rush to safety. The people of Aneyoshi heeded their historical marker and were saved in 2011. Christians read the book of Joshua, and all other Old Testament "holy war" texts, and heed the warning. They look to Jesus Christ, the Judge and Savior, the one with a "robe dipped in blood," and find safety.

But before we get to Jesus, the Old Testament introduces us to a different judge and savior: King David.

FROM JOSHUA TO DAVID

For the 200 years after Joshua led the Jewish people into the Promised Land, Israel is led by a series of judges, some of whom are wise, godly people, under whose leadership Israel does well, and others of whom are complete disasters. There is a prevailing sense of moral anarchy in Israel during this time. The book of Judges contains, but by no means condones, some truly horrific stories. The book ends with a sentence that sums up the moral temperature of the country: "In those days Israel had no king; everyone did as they saw fit" (Judges 21:25).

Israel suffers for lack of a leader, not only someone who will handle their economic, military, and domestic concerns, but someone who will also act as a moral leader, someone who will guide them in the way of the Lord. At the end of this two-hundred-year period after Joshua, God's people are in desperate need of a leader who will save them from themselves. It's now about 1000 BC.

From Joshua to David

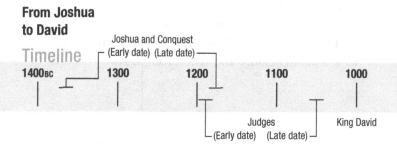

Timeline

Joshua and Conquest
(Early date) (Late date)

1400BC   1300   1200   1100   1000

Judges
(Early date)   (Late date)

King David

6

KINGDOM COME: THE PROMISE AND FAILURE OF KING DAVID

[DAVID,] YOUR HOUSE AND YOUR KINGDOM WILL ENDURE FOREVER BEFORE ME; YOUR THRONE WILL BE ESTABLISHED FOREVER.

(2 SAMUEL 7:16)

As we come to King David, the revered leader of Israel a thousand years before Christ, I want to confess that perhaps my most misconceived project as an author was presuming to write a book for the "Leadership" category of your local bookstore. I have been the singer in a band, a clergyman, an author and academic, and a media presenter; what would I really know about leading teams? Worse still, this particular book was on the subject of "humility." Who writes a book on leadership humility? The answer, to repeat the quip of a friend, is probably: someone with "the objective distance from the subject of humility." My publisher in the months before the book's release created a superb mock design, with my big face filling the cover, along with an alternative title, *"Humility and How I Achieved It."* It came with a glowing commendation on the cover—from John Dickson, of course! When they emailed it to me from their art department, I knew I was with the right publishing company.

The one real benefit of that project was being forced to read a lot of the genuine leadership literature on the market today. Some of it is brilliant. I was surprised at how much had been written exploring the counterintuitive dimensions of leadership. The most effective leaders are frequently mild-mannered. They put others first. They listen well to their team. And so on. These ideas are found in such esteemed sources as the *Harvard Business Review*. When you come across them, they seem almost obvious. Of course a good leader is a good listener! But these are *not* characteristics our society normally associates with corporate "greats" or with the military "top brass." And they are certainly not the qualities ancient societies looked for in leaders. Yet, as is often the case, the Bible takes an almost perverse delight in upending the paradigm of the leader. The narrative of King David reminds us that God's greatest victories often come to pass in unexpected ways, not according to the patterns of human power.

KING DAVID

David was not Israel's first king. That "honor"—though, as it turns out, it was more of a curse—fell to a man named Saul. And Saul *looked* like a king. He is said to be "as handsome a young man as could be found anywhere in Israel, and he was a head taller than anyone else" (1 Samuel 9:2). Given the Bible's delight in subverting human expectations of greatness, careful readers know that this cannot be a compliment! Many men, today and in antiquity, long to be a head taller than others! But while he looked the part, Saul was not a good king. He was deceitful, disobedient to God, and literally a madman. The narrative of 1 Samuel 9 – 15 is complicated, but the basic point is clear: the man Israel chose for their king turns out to be a disaster.

So, while Saul was still king, God sent the prophet Samuel to Bethlehem (yes, the same town in which Jesus is born a millennium later), a little town of no significance, to a family headed by a man named Jesse. Samuel's task was to find a king from among Jesse's eight sons. The seven oldest sons stood arrayed before Samuel as he observed that each them looked right for the job — handsome, strong, and kingly. But God told Samuel: "Do not consider his appearance or his height, for I have rejected him. The LORD does not look at the things people look at. People look at the outward appearance, but the LORD looks at the heart" (1 Samuel 16:7).

I was recently given a copy of *David and Goliath: Underdogs, Misfits and the Art of Battling Giants* (Allen Lane, 2013) by Malcolm Gladwell, the bestselling author of *Tipping Point*. It's an intriguing sociological account of how disadvantages often turn out to be advantages, and vice versa. I'm not sure I go along with many of Gladwell's biblical insights, but I was intrigued to find that 1 Samuel 16:7, just quoted, is the text he starts the book with: people look at the outward appearance, but the Lord looks at the heart. This is a key point of the narrative about David (and later about David's descendant Jesus).

Samuel examined all seven of Jesse's sons, and God rejected all of them, at which point Jesse revealed that he had another son, but he was young and unimpressive, just a shepherd—hardly royal material. This son, David, was brought before the prophet Samuel. It turns out this was the one God wanted. The Lord declared to his prophet: "Rise and anoint him; this is the one" (1 Samuel 16:12). Samuel anointed David—that is, he poured oil over his head as a sign that God had chosen him and marked him as the future king. While it was still some years before David is publicly recognized as king, he was preselected as the next ruler of Israel.

This secret anointing of David is more than a political act of subversion, and it is more than a morality tale on the importance of character over appearance; this story is hugely important, because it is the story of the first "messiah."

THE MESSIAH BEFORE JESUS

The word "anointed" that appears throughout the David story is the Hebrew word *mashiach*, or "messiah," the Greek equivalent of which is *christos*, or "Christ." In the Old Testament, all the kings were designated messiahs (christs) and were chosen by God to serve in the power of his Spirit. In Psalm 2 (from the so-called Wisdom Literature of the Bible), there is what many specialists believe to be part of an Israelite coronation ceremony. References to the king as God's "anointed" and his "son" are intriguing and inform the New Testament's way of speaking about Jesus (as we will see in chapter 8):

> The kings of the earth rise up
>   and the rulers band together
>   against the LORD and against his *anointed*, saying,

"Let us break their chains
>and throw off their shackles."

The One enthroned in heaven laughs;
>the Lord scoffs at them.

He rebukes them in his anger
>and terrifies them in his wrath, saying,

"I have installed my king
>on Zion, my holy mountain."

I will proclaim the LORD's decree:

He said to me, "You are my *son*;
>today I have become your father.

Ask me,
>and I will make the nations your inheritance,
>the ends of the earth your possession.
>>(Psalm 2:2 – 8, italics added)

The role of the messiah — the anointed son of God — was to save God's people. David did this time and again. He was a warrior king, famous for his military victories against Israel's enemies.

The narrative of David's secret anointing is followed immediately by two scenes in which David conquers evil by the power of the Spirit, which had come upon him. The first is understandably overlooked in contemporary talk about David — it certainly doesn't appear in Malcolm Gladwell's account. The second is one of the most famous stories in the Bible — and it forms the basis, metaphorically, of Gladwell's book. But *both* are highly significant for what the New Testament will later say about Jesus.

Scene 1. Having been anointed with the Spirit, the young David enters into the court of the reigning king Saul, who, by this time, is having a fit of madness. David, the shepherd and musician, brings relief to Saul *through music*:

> Now the Spirit of the LORD had departed from Saul, and an evil spirit from the LORD tormented him.
>
> Saul's attendants said to him, "See, an evil spirit from God is tormenting you. Let our lord command his servants here to search for someone who can play the lyre. He will play when the evil spirit from God comes on you, and you will feel better."...
>
> David came to Saul and entered his service. Saul liked him very much, and David became one of his armor-bearers.... Whenever the spirit from God came on Saul, David would take up his lyre and play. Then relief would come to Saul; he would feel better, and the evil spirit would leave him. (1 Samuel 16:14–23)

As odd as this story sounds, it creates a pattern for the "anointed one" that we will see reiterated in the life of Jesus, the great Anointed One. Just as David's first act as a "christ" was to conquer an "evil spirit," so Jesus' first act as *the* Christ, according to the Gospel of Mark, was to conquer the "devil" himself in a visionary encounter in the desert (Mark 1:12–13). More about that in chapter 8.

Scene 2. The clearest example of David's saving the people of God, which he does by relying not on his own powers but on the power of God, occurs in the next episode: the battle with Goliath. This story is so famous it has entered into vernacular. However, when we talk of a modern-day "David and Goliath battle," we usually just mean that an underdog triumphs over some giant adversary (metaphorically speaking) — this is the inspiration for Gladwell's book. But the point of the original David and Goliath story is not that David, the little guy, is the underdog who makes good; rather, the point is that *God* is the one who brings the victory to his anointed. According to the narrative, David and Goliath were so wildly unmatched it was ludicrous to expect the soon-to-be king to emerge the winner. The original account seems to have a little fun with the unimpressive nature of David:

> Then Saul dressed David in his own tunic. He put a coat of armor on him and a bronze helmet on his head. David fastened on his sword over the tunic and tried walking around, because he was not used to them.
>
> "I cannot go in these," he said to Saul, "because I am not used to them." So he took them off. Then he took his staff in his hand, chose five smooth stones from the stream, put them in the pouch of his shepherd's bag and, with his sling in his hand, approached the Philistine.
>
> Meanwhile, the Philistine, with his shield bearer in front of him, kept coming closer to David. He looked David over and saw that he was little more than a boy, glowing with health and handsome, and he despised him. He said to David, "Am I a dog, that you come at me with sticks?" And the Philistine cursed David by his gods. "Come here," he said, "and I'll give your flesh to the birds and the wild animals!"
>
> David said to the Philistine, "You come against me with sword and spear and javelin, but I come against you in the name of the LORD Almighty, the God of the armies of Israel, whom you have defied. This day the LORD will deliver you into my hands, and I'll strike you down and cut off your head. This very day I will give the carcasses of

the Philistine army to the birds and the wild animals, and the whole world will know that there is a God in Israel. All those gathered here will know that it is not by sword or spear that the LORD saves; for the battle is the LORD's, and he will give all of you into our hands."

As the Philistine moved closer to attack him, David ran quickly toward the battle line to meet him. Reaching into his bag and taking out a stone, he slung it and struck the Philistine on the forehead. The stone sank into his forehead, and he fell facedown on the ground. (1 Samuel 17:38 – 49)

Notice that before David goes out to fight Goliath, he tries on some armor, but it is too big and he cannot move in it, and so he goes without armor. David is given a sword, but he does not know how to use a sword, so he leaves the sword behind. Instead, David uses some rocks, a slingshot, and God's power to save the Israelites. I have stood in the valley of Elah, where the incident is said to have taken place. I've taken stones from the dried-up stream — for a scene for a TV documentary — and slung them from an ancient (style) sling. It is not easy. I'm glad most of the footage will never be seen!

This is the messianic story, the story of the anointed one, the christ, who will save God's people in unexpected ways. The Old Testament sets this up as an *eternal* story: Israel will be led by a series of messiahs as they wait and hope for a great Messiah, one like David but better, one who is *truly* a man after God's heart, who will lead God's people in power and peace and will do so without a sword (or even rocks and a sling).

ARCHAEOLOGY OF DAVID

Because of the striking nature of the story of David, a few Old Testament experts have doubted the king ever existed. It was never the majority view of specialists, but such skeptics argued that David is an ancient Jewish version of the "heroes" of Greece, such as Hercules and Achilles, about whom nothing historical can really be said. These scholars also point out that David is not mentioned by other ancient writings, outside of the Bible. There were no court records of Egypt or Syria decrying this omni-competent monarch—that is, until the early 1990s.

While investigating the region of Dan in the north of modern Israel, archaeologists in 1993–1994 uncovered a stele, a stone monument, which served as a piece of ancient propaganda. It was composed by Bar Hadad II, a king in Damascus, around the year 800 BC. In declaring his greatness in the face of his enemies, he mentions his superiority to "the house of David," a reference either to the dynasty of Davidic kings or to the city of his rule, Jerusalem. Either way, it is decent evidence, convincing most specialists that it is not plausible to think of David as a mythical character. He was as flesh-and-blood as Bar Hadad II. A friend of mine in Sydney, Dr. George Athas, has written an entire book on the Tel Dan inscription for those game enough to enter the sophisticated realm of Old Testament history and archaeology (George Athas, *The Tel Dan Inscription: A Reappraisal and a New Interpretation* [Sheffield Academic Press, 2003]).

BOOK NOTES From time to time popular writers, and even scholars, suggest that King David was a pure invention of a later time in Israel's history, that he was an "idealized" king created to serve as the founding hero of Israel's kingdom. The argument is intrinsically problematic, to put it politely, not least because of the warts-and-all way in which David's weaknesses and gross sins are laid bare for all to see. A more scholarly answer to the question of the "historical David," however, can be found in the book edited by the Scottish Old Testament professor (now at Regent College, Vancouver) Iain Provan, *A Biblical History of Israel* (Westminster John Knox, 2003), 193–232.

THE PARADOX OF THE MESSIAHS

When David eventually goes public and Israel hails him as king, God makes an extraordinary promise to him through the prophet Nathan. Its significance for the biblical story cannot be overstated. David is said to be starting something "eternal":

> "The LORD declares to you that the LORD himself will establish a house for you: When your days are over and you rest with your ancestors, I will raise up your offspring to succeed you, your own flesh and blood, and I will establish his kingdom. He is the one who will build a house for my Name, and I will establish the throne of his kingdom forever. I will be his father, and he will be my son. When he does wrong, I will punish him with a rod wielded by men, with floggings inflicted by human hands. But my love will never be taken away from him,

as I took it away from Saul, whom I removed from before you. Your house and your kingdom will endure forever before me; your throne will be established forever." (2 Samuel 7:11b–16)

Here God promises to establish a line of messiah-kings whom he will discipline but from whom he will never remove his love and favor. This promise marks a great moment for Israel as they begin to hope that, come what may, their vision of a messiah will last forever.

However, the Israelite messiah-kings present us with a profound paradox. It is the paradox of the entire Old Testament. These kings are chosen by God and anointed with his power, but they are also spectacularly sinful. These are not uber-kings, infallible and almighty; some of them are far from moral examples to us.

King David himself, Israel's greatest king, commits adultery, and after finding his mistress, Bathsheba, pregnant, he organizes to have her husband murdered so that no one will find out what he has done. But the prophet Nathan confronts David, accusing him of a gross departure from the ways of God. Instead of having the prophet "royally removed," as many an ancient monarch would have done, David breaks down and admits his wrongdoing, enters a time of profound contrition, and even allows his story to enter the official annals of Israelite history—which is why we know about it at all.

Having been a musician all his life, David composes a song, one of the 150 songs that make up the book of Psalms. It is a powerful statement of the ugliness of the human heart and of the mercy of God's heart. When I need reminding of either or both of these themes, I find myself turning to these words and saying them out loud to my Maker:

> Have mercy on me, O God,
>> according to your unfailing love;
> according to your great compassion
>> blot out my transgressions.
> Wash away all my iniquity
>> and cleanse me from my sin....
> Cleanse me with hyssop, and I will be clean;
>> wash me, and I will be whiter than snow.
> Let me hear joy and gladness;
>> let the bones you have crushed rejoice.
> Hide your face from my sins
>> and blot out all my iniquity.
> Create in me a pure heart, O God,
>> and renew a steadfast spirit within me.
> Do not cast me from your presence
>> or take your Holy Spirit from me.
> Restore to me the joy of your salvation
>> and grant me a willing spirit, to sustain me....
> You do not delight in sacrifice, or I would bring it;
>> you do not take pleasure in burnt offerings.
> My sacrifice, O God, is a broken spirit;
>> a broken and contrite heart
>> you, God, will not despise. (Psalm 51:1 – 17)

I once quoted this psalm in full in a prematch speech to an American NFL team (it's a long story how I got to do that!). Here were thirty or so giant men — tough, David-like men, on salaries a hundred times my own — but I got the real sense that all of them knew the reality of the human heart. You can appear to have everything, enjoy the praise of everyone, but know in your heart that your thoughts, words, and deeds don't meet your own standards, let alone those of the Almighty.

Here is the paradox of the kings, and indeed the paradox of the entire Old Testament: this sinful family line, this sinful nation, will never have the love of God taken away, and God will establish a kingdom *forever* through the faulty lineage of David. As the prophet Nathan declared on God's behalf, "Your throne will be established forever" (2 Samuel 7:16).

The narrative of the Old Testament is peppered with unappealing, almost embarrassing heroes like David and the kings who follow him. Why? Because, ultimately, the Old Testament is not really about these fellows. The Bible is not interested in hagiographies, stories about the intrinsic "holiness" of their heroes; it is interested in telling the account of *God's grace* to fallen humanity. We are all "Adam" — even the kings of Israel — but the Creator has good intentions and affection toward us.

FAILURES OF THE KINGS

Quite unlike any national history of antiquity that I know of, the Old Testament writers almost delight in telling you how sinful their nation is and how sinful their heroes and kings are, and yet how merciful God is toward the nation. I have never seen this approach to historical writing in anything I've come across in the literature of Egypt, Babylon, Greece, or Rome. But these are the twin themes of the rest of the Old Testament: the *failure* of even the best of God's people and the *patient love* of God himself.

For the next four hundred years—the next two hundred pages of the Bible—we see the kings of Israel, and the nation itself, flip-flopping between periods of partial obedience and longer periods of disobedience, injustice, neglect of the poor, the worship of idols, and so on.

The spiral of wrongdoing culminates in the tragic downfall of Israel. In 722 BC the north of Israel (usually just called "Israel") collapses under the Assyrians, and in 586 BC the south (called "Judah") is conquered by the Babylonians. The biblical perspective is that these are not mere sociopolitical events; they are God's discipline of his own wayward people. The Old Testament puts this in no uncertain terms. At the close of the royal period (from 1000 BC to 586 BC) we read:

> All this took place because the Israelites had sinned against the LORD their God, who had brought them up out of Egypt from under the power of Pharaoh king of Egypt. They worshiped other gods and followed the practices of the nations the LORD had driven out before them, as well as the practices that the kings of Israel had introduced.... The LORD warned Israel and Judah through all his prophets and seers: "Turn from your evil ways. Observe my commands and decrees, in accordance with the entire Law that I commanded your ancestors to obey and that I delivered to you through my servants the prophets."
>
> But they would not listen and were as stiff-necked as their ancestors, who did not trust in the LORD their God....
>
> They forsook all the commands of the LORD their God and made for themselves two idols cast in the shape of calves, and an Asherah pole. They bowed down to all

the starry hosts, and they worshiped Baal. They sacrificed their sons and daughters in the fire. They practiced divination and sought omens and sold themselves to do evil in the eyes of the LORD, arousing his anger.

So the LORD was very angry with Israel and removed them from his presence. Only the tribe of Judah was left, and even Judah did not keep the commands of the LORD their God. They followed the practices Israel had introduced. Therefore the LORD rejected all the people of Israel; he afflicted them and gave them into the hands of plunderers, until he thrust them from his presence (2 Kings 17:7 – 20).

Four hundred years of royal history in four paragraphs — that's how the Bible describes the demise of Israel. And it sounds a lot like Adam in the garden, as many have pointed out. As I mentioned in chapter 1, Adam was given a beautiful strip of land and was told to obey God's law. When he defied the Almighty, he was expelled, exiled, from the garden and from the presence of God. Adam's story is a preview of the story of Israel, a nation in exile, thrust from the Promised Land for defying God's good law.

PROMISES OF THE KINGDOM

But alongside this terrible theme of the spiral of disobedience and judgment stands the other great theme. Through this whole period of disobedience, the prophets mentioned in the passage above not only warned of Israel's judgment, but they also promised restoration, a return from exile, and the establishment of David's eternal kingdom. This is what the next two hundred or more pages of the Old Testament are about, the writings of the prophets—Isaiah, Jeremiah, Ezekiel, Joel, Amos, and the rest.

The writings of the prophets record both warnings of judgment and promises of renewal. In short, the prophets said, "You're disobedient, but God's love will not be taken away. The kingdom will be established. Your sin cannot triumph over God's promises of grace." (I would say this is the punch line of the entire Old Testament: mercy trumps sin).

According to the prophets, out of the rubbish heap that was Israel in the sixth century BC, a descendant from Jesse, the family name of David, would come the Messiah—now with a capital "M." The prophet Micah speaks of a ruler from Bethlehem: "But you, Bethlehem Ephrathah, though you are small among the clans of Judah, out of you will come for me one who will be ruler over Israel, whose origins are from of old" (Micah 5:2). Five hundred or so years later, of course, the Gospels would say that Jesus, the descendant of David, was born in lowly Bethlehem.

From around 700 BC, another famous prophet, Isaiah, looked forward to a "great light" that would emerge not from down south in Bethlehem but up north in Galilee. The light was a person, we're told, a "Prince of Peace," whose rule will know no end and no bounds:

> The people walking in darkness
> > have seen a great light;
> on those living in the land of deep darkness
> > a light has dawned....
> For to us a child is born,
> > to us a son is given,

> and the government will be on his shoulders.
> And he will be called
>> Wonderful Counselor, Mighty God,
>> Everlasting Father, Prince of Peace.
> Of the greatness of his government and peace
>> there will be no end.
> He will reign on David's throne
>> and over his kingdom,
> establishing and upholding it
>> with justice and righteousness
>> from that time on and forever. (Isaiah 9:2–7)

The Lord of the world will come from Galilee. I will say more about this in the next chapter, but it is worth pausing to ponder how unlikely a promise this really is. Galilee was the region recently (from Isaiah's perspective) destroyed and repopulated with Gentiles—non-Jews—and, as the centuries rolled on, the region continued to be the butt of jokes and insults, despite this prophetic forecast. *Can anything good come out of Galilee?* it was sometimes asked. As is well known, seven hundred years later Jesus' home district was Nazareth of Galilee, and the majority of his ministry was conducted throughout the towns of Galilee. More about that later.

A couple of chapters later, Isaiah speaks once again of this omni-powerful descendant of David, the Messiah with a capital "M":

> A shoot will come up from the stump of Jesse [David's
>> family],
>> from his roots a Branch will bear fruit.
> The Spirit of the LORD will rest on him [an "anointing"]—
>> the Spirit of wisdom and of understanding,

> the Spirit of counsel and of might,
> the Spirit of knowledge and fear of the LORD —
> and he will delight in the fear of the LORD.
> He will not judge by what he sees with his eyes
> or decide by what he hears with his ears,
> but with righteousness he will judge the needy,
> with justice he will give decisions for the poor of
> the earth....

In that day the Root of Jesse will stand as a banner for the peoples; the nations will rally to him. (Isaiah 11:1 – 10)

Especially significant is the mention of the "nations" in this prophecy. It may seem a long time ago (in this book, and in the Old Testament itself) that the promise to Abraham emphasized how "all peoples on earth will be blessed through you" (Genesis 12:3), but ancient prophets like Isaiah never forgot that God's dealings with their little nation would (one day) have huge implications for the entire world. Not only will Israel return from its exile, but "the nations will rally" around a descendant of Abraham and of David, the Anointed One.

To this day, our Orthodox Jewish friends await this descendant of David who will rule the nations in justice and peace. A traditional Jewish daily prayer from the Siddur, the Jewish prayer book, reads: "Have mercy, our God, on Israel Your people; on Jerusalem Your city, on Zion the resting place of Your Glory, on the monarchy of the house of David, Your Messiah" (*Rahem*, Third Blessing after Meals). All of this reveals the scandal at the heart of the New Testament, which will identify Jesus of Nazareth as this long-awaited Messiah.

As we come to the end of our treatment of the *Old* Testament, let me summarize its message in a nutshell. Put simply, the Old Testament assures us that where sin abounds, grace abounds all the more. Where God's people fail, God's promises will prevail. God's people, the Old Testament says again and again, need a deliverer sent from God. They need a *perfect* Messiah. And God in his love will do just that. Through this descendant of David the spiritual, social, and physical aspects of our existence, established in Eden and temporarily recaptured in Israel's Promised Land, will be restored and fully realized. That is what the *New* Testament is about.

FROM THE END OF THE OLD TESTAMENT TO THE TIME OF THE ROMANS AND THE NEW TESTAMENT

The final book of the Old Testament is Malachi, which contains the message of God to the Israelites after they had been exiled from the land and after some had returned to Jerusalem to rebuild the mess. At this point, Israel was in a dark place, but among the prophecies made by Malachi was this wonderful promise from God: "But for you who revere my name, the sun of righteousness will rise with healing in its rays. And you will go out and frolic like well-fed calves" (Malachi 4:2). The book ends—and therefore the whole Old Testament ends—with a prophecy of a messenger who will get everyone ready for the appearance of the mighty Lord himself:

> See, I will send the prophet Elijah to you before that great and dreadful day of the LORD comes. He will turn the hearts of the parents to their children, and

the hearts of the children to their parents; or else I will come and strike the land with total destruction. (Malachi 4:5–6)

Elijah was a hugely influential prophet around 800 BC (i.e., three hundred years before Malachi). Malachi's prophecy says that a new "Elijah-like" figure will come and prepare people for God's own arrival. The mention of turning parents to children and children to parents has nothing to do with better family relationships; it refers to the central responsibility of Jewish parents to teach their offspring about the promises and ways of Israel's God. These lines, then, are about a total turning back to the paths of God. The words "or else" in the final clause could imply that the Old Testament ends on a downer, with a warning of judgment. Older translations use the archaic term "lest," which I think captures the sense better. "Lest" means "so that not." This Elijah-like messenger is sent prior to the arrival of God himself so that he would not come in judgment. The last line of Malachi—the final line of the Old Testament—is less a threat of judgment than a statement of God's intention to avert judgment.

On that note, the Old Testament closes and Israel is left waiting. The Bible is silent for almost five hundred years in what is known as the intertestamental period. A lot happens in history during that time—the Greeks rule, the Romans rise to power and take over pretty much everything—but, from God's point of view, the most significant thing to happen in the next half millennium is the birth of a child in relative obscurity. This would not be the first time God had chosen to effect magisterial plans through unexpectedly ignoble circumstances, but this would undoubtedly be the most significant.

From the End of the Old Testament to the Time of the Romans and the New Testament

430 BC	
420	
410	
400	Malachi c. 430 BC
390	
380	
370	
360	
350	
340	
330	334–323 Alexander the Great conquers the East
320	330–328 Alexander's years of power
310	320 Ptolemy (I) Soter conquers Jerusalem
300	311 Seleucus conquers Babylon; Seleucid dynasty begins
290	
280	
270	
260	
250	
240	
230	
220	226 Antiochus (III) of Syria conquers the Holy Land
210	223–187 Antiochus becomes Seleucid ruler of Syria
200	198 Antiochus defeats Egypt and gains control of the Holy Land
190	175–164 Antiochus (IV) Epiphanes rules Syria; Judaism is prohibited
180	
170	167 Mattathia and his sons rebel against Antiochus; Maccabean revolt begins
160	166-160 Judas Maccabeus's leadership
150	160–143 Jonathan is high priest
140	142–134 Simon becomes high priest; establishes Hasmonean dynasty
130	
120	134–104 John Hyrcanus enlarges the independent Jewish state
110	
100	103 Aristobulus's rule
90	102–76 Alexander Janneus's rule
80	75–67 Rule of Salome Alexandra with Hyrcanus II as high priest
70	
60	66–63 Battle between Aristobulus II and Hyrcanus II
50	63 Pompey invades the Holy Land; Roman rule begins
40	63–40 Hyrcanus II governs but is subject to Rome
30	40–37 Parthians conquer Jerusalem
20	37 Herod becomes ruler of the Holy Land
10	19 Herod's temple begun
10 AD	4 Herod dies; Archelaus succeeds him
20	
30	

7

HOPE AGAINST HOPE:
THE CHRISTMAS STORY

TODAY IN THE TOWN OF DAVID A SAVIOR HAS BEEN BORN TO YOU; HE IS
THE MESSIAH, THE LORD. THIS WILL BE A SIGN TO YOU: YOU WILL FIND
A BABY WRAPPED IN CLOTHS AND LYING IN A MANGER.

(LUKE 2:11 – 12)

For some, the West's continued attachment to the Christmas story, with its guiding stars, wise men from the East, angelic announcements, and a baby laid in a manger, is evidence of the human capacity for self-deception, of believing things contrary to all the evidence. If you've ever read God's favorite atheists Richard Dawkins or Christopher Hitchens on this theme, you will know exactly what I mean.

Admittedly, on first blush, the New Testament Christmas narrative does open with some far-fetched stories. There's nothing like reading the original narratives for yourself. First, here's the account in the Gospel of Luke:

> In those days Caesar Augustus issued a decree that a census should be taken of the entire Roman world. (This

was the first census that took place while Quirinius was governor of Syria.) And everyone went to their own town to register.

So Joseph also went up from the town of Nazareth in Galilee to Judea, to Bethlehem the town of David, because he belonged to the house and line of David. He went there to register with Mary, who was pledged to be married to him and was expecting a child. While they were there, the time came for the baby to be born, and she gave birth to her firstborn, a son. She wrapped him in cloths and placed him in a manger, because there was no guest room available for them.

And there were shepherds living out in the fields nearby, keeping watch over their flocks at night. An angel of the Lord appeared to them, and the glory of the Lord shone around them, and they were terrified. But the angel said to them, "Do not be afraid. I bring you good news that will cause great joy for all the people. Today in the town of David a Savior has been born to you; he is the Messiah, the Lord. This will be a sign to you: You will find a baby wrapped in cloths and lying in a manger."

Suddenly a great company of the heavenly host appeared with the angel, praising God and saying,

"Glory to God in the highest heaven,
    and on earth peace to those on whom his favor
    rests." (Luke 2:1 – 14)

It is the Gospel of Matthew that contains the story of the wandering star and the three wise kings (well, several "Magi" at least):

After Jesus was born in Bethlehem in Judea, during the time of King Herod, Magi from the east came to Jerusalem and asked, "Where is the one who has been born king of the Jews? We saw his star when it rose and have come to worship him."

When King Herod heard this he was disturbed, and all Jerusalem with him. When he had called together all the people's chief priests and teachers of the law, he asked them where the Messiah was to be born. "In Bethlehem in Judea," they replied, "for this is what the prophet has written:

"'But you, Bethlehem, in the land of Judah,
       are by no means least among the rulers of Judah;
 for out of you will come a ruler
       who will shepherd my people Israel.'"

... After they [the Magi] had heard the king, they went on their way, and the star they had seen when it rose went ahead of them until it stopped over the place where the child was. When they saw the star, they were overjoyed. On coming to the house, they saw the child with his mother Mary, and they bowed down and worshiped him. Then they opened their treasures and presented him with gifts of gold, frankincense and myrrh. (Matthew 2:1–11)

Richard Dawkins and others pour scorn on the West's fixation with this story and all of the traditions that have grown up around it.

Part of me wants to counter such skepticism with a "history lesson," pointing out the unusual degree of evidence we have for the life of Jesus—which is why you can do a history course on Jesus at university, just as you can do one on Alexander the Great or Julius Caesar (I teach one at the University of Sydney). But I've written enough books on purely historical questions, and I'll leave it to readers to explore them at their leisure.

BOOK NOTES

Scholarly books on the historical Jesus are numerous, probably more numerous than all of the scholarly books on Julius Caesar and Alexander the Great combined. This makes it difficult for the general reader to have a clear sense of the "landscape" of the field. When there are this many books on a topic, just about every bias and preconception is satisfied: you can always find a book to say what you want it to say. Skeptics can find books arguing that Jesus never lived (though they're usually not books written by professors of history), and fundamentalist Christians can find books "proving" everything in the Gospels' accounts of his life (again, usually not written by professors of history). Unless someone has read at least twenty of the hundreds of important books on the topic, I think it is unlikely they will have a clear sense of what the scholarly mainstream is really saying about Jesus.

Unfortunately, websites like Wikipedia rarely accurately describe the contours of so complex a field. My best efforts to offer an "informed journalistic account" of mainstream scholarship on Jesus are found in three of my books: the historical sources and methods are discussed in *Investigating Jesus: An Historian's Quest* (Lion Hudson, 2010), or the simpler and briefer *The Christ Files: How Historians Know What They Know about Jesus* (Zondervan, 2010); what those sources and methods confirm about Jesus' actual life and ministry is described in *Jesus: A*

Short Life (Lion Hudson, 2008—try and get the picture-book version). For the fearless, my favorite book on the topic by a top-tier scholar remains that of Professor James Dunn of Durham University, *Jesus Remembered* (Eerdmans, 2003).

My other response to the charge of self-deception is to point out that self-deception, in the sense of accepting things that seem unbelievable, is not always a bad thing! Some of the most beautiful and real things are also the most seemingly preposterous.

There's some interesting research on this theme. In *I Told Me So* American philosopher Gregg Elshof explores the ubiquitous nature of self-deception in public and private life. I squirmed from the opening lines: "A mother somehow manages not to notice the obvious signs that her son is on drugs. A wife does the same with respect to her husband's affair. All of the evidence is easily available. Yet it goes unseen" (*I Told Me So* [Eerdmans, 2009], 1). Research uncovers how common self-deception is among the young and old, rich and poor, students and professors. One of the delightfully disturbing studies found that 94 percent of professors believe they are doing a "better-than-average job"! It seems we have an amazing ability not to let the facts get in the way of our own story of ourselves.

But that's not the end of it. Elshof also explores the great good that often comes from telling ourselves things that don't seem to be true. We might call this self-deception, but it could just as easily be called "hope against hope." The same human trait that allows a politician to convince

127

himself his "lofty ends" justify his dodgy means, also allows a powerless black female activist, like Rosa Parks, to believe against all the evidence that civil rights were coming to Alabama. Though at the time she was arrested for not giving up her seat to a white man on a bus, she lived to see her impossible dream come true.

Self-deception has an upside. It allows us to dare to imagine the impossible and frequently to watch it unfold. It is the key to hope against hope! Viktor Frankl, in his famous psychological reflections on Auschwitz, observed that self-deception (the ability to sideline the evidence) made survival in the death camps possible for many. He compares it to "the delusion of reprieve" observed in some death-row prisoners who, right up to the end, believe they will be found innocent. In Auschwitz, Frankl said, this happy self-deception gave people hope, a reason to live, and it saved lives. Or think of Nelson Mandela in his Robben Island prison. What enabled him to believe—for twenty-seven long years—not only that he would one day be free but that the nation that left him to rot would be transformed by nonviolence, reconciliation, and love, and then make him their president? It certainly wasn't "evidence" that sustained him. It was a noble ability to sideline the evidence and hope against hope—a kind of prophetic madness that only looks like genius in retrospect.

Yes, there are preposterous elements in the story of the birth of Jesus—guiding stars, a virgin birth, angelic hosts, not to mention the promise of "peace on earth." But I am more interested here in the equally bizarre bits placed alongside the miracles of the story. Miracle stories are often used to enhance the greatness of a figure — to hide anything ordinary about the hero. But in the Jesus story, miracles are set in obvious juxtaposition with a shocking *ordinariness* of the Messiah. Miracles don't hide the meekness of the story; they emphasize it. However hard it is to believe in a virgin birth and angelic visitations, it is just as hard to get our heads around the central themes of Christmas. The long-awaited King is born in almost total obscurity. The God of the universe is wrapped in swaddling cloths. The one who would become history's most revered name — whose follow-ers knew in their bones this would be so — began life where the goats fed and relieved themselves, a manger.

Inevitably, many will continue to think of Christmas as delusional, akin to believing in "fairies at the bottom of the garden," "flying spaghetti monsters," and all that. But I think of Christmas as the ultimate expression of hope against hope, of self-deception of the healthy kind. The Christmas story is a Mandela-like prophetic madness that turns out to be true genius. Indeed, Mandela himself made just such a connection in a 1992 speech (still on the ANC website). Mandela explicitly said that the story of Jesus, cli-maxing in his death and resurrection, fueled his own confi-dence that humility and love could — despite all evidence to the contrary — overcome power and violence:

> Our Messiah, who came to us in the form of a mortal man, but who by his suffering and crucifixion attained immortality. Our Messiah, born like an outcast in a sta-ble, and executed like a criminal on the cross. Our Mes-siah, whose life bears testimony to the truth that there is no shame in poverty: Those who should be ashamed are

they who impoverish others. Whose life testifies to the truth that there is no shame in being persecuted: Those who should be shamed are they who persecute others. Whose life proclaims the truth that there is no shame in being conquered: Those who should be ashamed are they who conquer others. Whose life testifies to the truth that there is no shame in being dispossessed: Those who should be ashamed are they who dispossess others. Whose life testifies to the truth that there is no shame in being oppressed: Those who should be ashamed are they who oppress others. (Speech given in Moria, April 3, 1994)

In the decade that followed, Mandela, who had formerly advocated violent resistance, watched his dream of transformation through love come true. What to many must have seemed like a "self-deception" through the quarter century leading up to his release from prison became one of the most tangible good news stories of the twentieth century.

The birth of Jesus, with all of its miraculous, ignoble, unbelievable elements, has all of the hallmarks of Mandela-like prophetic genius, daring us to follow our hunch that there's more to life than meets the eye — life beyond the death camp, a future beyond Robben Island. It asks us to imagine that pure Majesty has come for us in great humility. It allows us to hope that despite our infinitesimal place in the universe and profound moral failings, God loves us.

As Jesus reached adulthood, this prophetic genius would come to full flourishing.

8

THE WAIT IS OVER (ALMOST): JESUS AND HIS GOSPEL

JESUS WENT INTO GALILEE, PROCLAIMING THE GOOD NEWS OF GOD. "THE TIME HAS COME," HE SAID. "THE KINGDOM OF GOD HAS COME NEAR. REPENT AND BELIEVE THE GOOD NEWS!"

(MARK 1:14 – 15)

I have written several books on the history and significance of Jesus, so I don't intend here to outline the main events of his life or to emphasize what he means to me personally (as much as I would love to think readers will choose to explore these themes). Instead, I want to take one key passage from one of the accounts of his life and provide an example of how deeply rooted the Jesus story is in the Old Testament. The Old and the New Testaments are not two unrelated narratives clunkily joined together. Jesus Christ is the climax of God's covenant with Israel: that's the claim I want to explore. Only at the end of the chapter will I provide a kind of "crib notes" to the life of Jesus, with a series of readings from the Gospels that likewise present Christ as the fulfillment of the hopes of Israel.

But, first, what are these Gospels?

THE GOSPELS

The New Testament starts with the four Gospels, four biographies of Jesus' life. Recent research has emphasized the remarkable resemblance between these four books and other biographies of great men written around the same time. Two gospels were written by disciples (Matthew and John), a third comes from a physician and colleague of the apostle Paul (Luke), and the fourth is by the hand of the secretary and translator of the apostle Peter (Mark). These four Gospels contain the triumphant news that the Messiah has come to restore the spiritual, social, and environmental brokenness of the world. The wait is over: almost.

The four accounts of Jesus' life are called "gospels" for a reason. "Gospel" means "good (or grand) news," and it is a word freighted with meaning. While today we are used to hearing it used in Christian parlance, "gospel" was a word with a long history in both Greco-Roman and Jewish cultures.

ARCHAEOLOGY OF "GOSPEL"

One powerful example of the pre-Christian usage of the term "gospel" comes from a decree dating to just before the birth of Jesus. It was common to announce important or surprising events, especially ones relating to great leaders, as "gospels." The military victories of generals, significant weddings, and the ascensions to the throne of the emperors Gaius Caligula and Vespasian—these were all formally declared as gospels. A particularly important example is the decree of Paulus Fabius Maximus, an official in the eastern part of the Roman empire, demanding that Emperor Augustus should be honored for his great achievements—for the good news or "gospels" he brought to the world—by resetting the official calendar so that it coincided with his year of birth (63 BC). The decree made in 9 BC was proclaimed throughout the region and inscribed on stone monuments in public places. One such inscription has since been uncovered in Priene in southwest Turkey. It reads as follows:

> Augustus has made war to cease and put everything in peaceful order; and, whereas the birthday of our god [the emperor] signalled the beginning of gospels for the world because of him, Paulus Fabius Maximus, benefactor of the province, has discovered a way to honor Augustus that was hitherto unknown among the Greeks, namely, to reckon time from the date of his birth. (*Orientis Graeci Inscriptiones*, 2:458)

The resetting of a calendar around the date of birth of a universally important figure has some resonance with the decision five hundred or so years later to "reckon time" from the date of Jesus' birth—most of us have forgotten Emperor Augustus, but we use BC ("before Christ") and AD (*anno domini*, "in the year of the Lord") on a nearly daily basis. More striking is the way "gospel" is used in this inscription. Augustus, described here as divine, brought peace into a world in great torment. His achievement was the cause of many gospels that, as a result, have spread throughout the world. The historical reach of gospels about Augustus, however, pales in comparison to that of the gospel of Jesus Christ.

"Gospel" was a Jewish word long before it was a Christian (or Greco-Roman) word. In fact, the little word "gospel" is one of the great bridges between the Old and the New Testament: gospel is what the whole Old Testament looked forward to.

The prophet Isaiah, centuries before Christ, looked forward to heralds who would one day bring a gospel of God's reign as king, his kingdom:

> How beautiful on the mountains
>   are the feet of those who bring good news [*gospel*],
> who proclaim peace,
>   who bring good tidings [*gospel*],
>   who proclaim salvation,
> who say to Zion,
>   "Your God reigns!" (Isaiah 52:7)

The same prophet also spoke of an anointed king who would come and declare a gospel:

> The Spirit of the Sovereign LORD is on me
>   because the LORD has anointed me [the verb of
>   the word "messiah"]
>   to proclaim good news [*gospel*] to the poor.
> He has sent me to bind up the brokenhearted,
>   to proclaim freedom for the captives

> and release from darkness for the prisoners
> to proclaim the year of the LORD's favor. (Isaiah 61:1–2)

The New Testament says it is Jesus who brings the good news, the gospel, as promised in the Old Testament. The writers of the Gospels try to make it plain that they are not simply telling the story of a great man and his teachings. They are telling the news of the prophesied, longed-for Messiah or Christ.

In different ways, all four Gospels make the point that Jesus is the fulfillment of the "gospel" heralded for centuries in the Old Testament—a gospel that would also eclipse the "gospels" of Rome. As we slow down in this long chapter to look at the first few paragraphs of Mark, we will see just how subtle and sophisticated this program is, as Mark offers an extraordinary interweaving of Old Testament words and themes to tell us the biography of Jesus.

MARK AND THE BEGINNING OF THE GOSPEL

The Gospels of Matthew and Luke use their Christmas narratives to draw out the connections between Jesus and the promises of the Old Testament. Mark bypasses Jesus' birth and childhood entirely and commences his narrative around the year AD 28 with the strange figure of John the Baptist and the fully grown Jesus of Nazareth. In these few short paragraphs Mark is able to emphasize that, with the coming of Jesus, the wait is over: the blessings promised to Abraham and the kingdom of God promised to David have arrived—well, *pretty much* arrived.

Mark hits us from the opening line, which functions more like a title of the work than its first sentence: "The beginning of the good news about Jesus the Messiah, the Son of God" (Mark 1:1). The line is packed with Old Testament flavor. The word "good news/gospel," as we have just seen, is a crucial Old Testament term for the good news of God's climactic dealings with the world in fulfillment of his ancient promises. For anyone aware of this background, these words would have inspired excitement or skepticism, perhaps both.

Then there's the word "Messiah/Christ": this is "the gospel about Jesus the Messiah." When I was a child, I thought "Christ" was his surname. I imagined that Joseph Christ married Mary, and they had a whole lot of little baby Christs, the firstborn of whom was Jesus Christ. But we have seen that Christ is a *title*, not a surname. It is the Greek translation of the Hebrew *Mashiach* or Messiah, which means the "anointed one," the one chosen and empowered to save, just like King David a thousand years before (discussed in chapter 6).

Mark adds the title "Son of God." It is an expression employed in the Old Testament for ancient Israelite kings. As those who ruled on God's behalf, they were like "sons" to the Almighty. As I said in chapter 6, one of the psalms of the Old Testament seems to have retained lines from an Israelite coronation ceremony:

> I have installed my king
> on Zion, my holy mountain.
> I will proclaim the LORD's decree:
> He said to me, "You are my son;
> today I have become your father." (Psalm 2:6–7)

Ancient Roman readers of Mark's gospel would have had an additional thought as they read the words "Son of God" in his opening line. Many of the silver coins of the time heralded the emperor as a "son of god." As I type these words, I am wearing a silver denarius on a necklace; it was in circulation at the time of Jesus. Tiberius, the emperor from AD 14 – 37, appears on the front (the obverse) and his mother, Livia, is stamped on the back (the reverse). Around the imperial image in tiny Latin script are inscribed the words *divi filius*, "son of god." It is a reference to Tiberius's status as the son of the divinized Emperor Augustus (who was the adoptive son of Julius Caesar and regarded as the founder of imperial Rome). The claim of Mark's gospel that Jesus was the Son of God would have struck Roman readers as bold, perhaps even subversive. And I doubt Mark would have been happy with anything less. For him, the descendant of King David was indeed the true king of the world. The Caesars were mere human, temporary appointments.

Mark makes use of this opening title "Son of God" in another significant portion of his biography—right toward the end. In Mark 15, when Jesus hangs crucified by order of the Roman authorities, a Roman centurion somehow perceives Jesus' hidden majesty and declares, "Surely this man was the Son of God!" (Mark 15:39). It is a striking moment in the narrative, as a representative of Rome's earthly power sees in the teacher, healer, and martyr from Galilee the true Lord. All notions of greatness are thereby overturned. This "Son of God" would rule not through coinage or armies but through his death for the sins of the world, for Jews and for Romans, for the descendants of Abraham and for all the nations. It is a specific point Jesus himself made in the middle of Mark's gospel. Contrasting Roman rule with his own, he remarked:

> You know that those who are regarded as rulers of the Gentiles lord it over them, and their high officials exercise authority over them. Not so with you. Instead, whoever wants to become great among you must be your servant, and whoever wants to be first must be slave of all. For even the Son of Man [Jesus' circumlocution for himself] did not come to be served, but to serve, and to give his life as a ransom for many. (Mark 10:42–45)

Not everyone has appreciated this reversal of notions of power. The great nineteenth-century atheist Friedrich Nietzsche damned Christianity at just this point. In *The Anti-Christ* he opines that "the case of the death of the Nazarene" is the high point (or low point) of the absurd and unhealthy "religion of pity": "Christianity has taken the side of everything weak, base, ill-constituted.... [It] thwarts the law of evolution, the law of selection. It preserves what is ripe for destruction; it defends life's condemned" (Friedrich Nietzsche, *Twilight of Idols / The Anti-Christ* [Penguin Books, 1990], 129–30). A generation later Adolf Hitler felt the same. In Richard Steigmann-Gall's subtle and disturbing account of Hitler's complex relationship with Christianity, he shows how Nazism "despised Christian meekness and humility," even while (somehow) co-opting Jesus as the Aryan forebear of the German struggle against the Jews (*The Holy Reich: Nazi Conceptions of Christianity, 1919–1945* [Cambridge University Press, 2005], 262).

When Mark tells us in his opening line that this gospel

is about the "Son of God," he does not mean merely that his story concerns a leader more powerful than Israelite kings and Roman emperors; he means that this Jesus embodies a new and superior notion of rule entirely. It is not earthly, human rule at all, but the loving rule of God that comes to serve our deepest need (forgiveness of sin). The death of Jesus — the climax of all four Gospels — becomes the moment of greatest victory, for it is through this event that people from every nation may be forgiven and restored to their Maker, just as the Old Testament promised. In the course of history, this is precisely what happens, as countless millions from every corner of the world find themselves drawn to, and liberated by, the crucified Son of God.

This paradigm shift in notions of power and rule will require some preparation, and Mark's next few lines — as we wind back to the beginning of the gospel — introduce us not yet to Jesus but to the one sent to prepare his way.

JOHN THE PREPARER

Following the "title" as just explored, Mark's work proper begins with a quotation from the Old Testament:

> It is written in Isaiah the prophet:
>
>> "I will send my messenger ahead of you
>>> who will prepare your way" —
>> "a voice of one calling in the wilderness,
>> 'Prepare the way for the Lord,
>>> make straight paths for him.'" (Mark 1:2–3)

Jewish tradition expected a great preparer to herald

the arrival of the Lord. Indeed, in chapter 6 I pointed out that the Old Testament ends with that expectation: "I will send the prophet Elijah to you before that great and dreadful day of the LORD comes" (Malachi 4:5). In the following paragraph of the gospel, Mark tells us that the long-expected preparer — the Elijah figure — arrived in the person of John the Baptist:

> And so John the Baptist appeared in the wilderness, preaching a baptism of repentance for the forgiveness of sins. The whole Judean countryside and all the people of Jerusalem went out to him. Confessing their sins, they were baptized by him in the Jordan River. John wore clothing made of camel's hair, with a leather belt around his waist, and he ate locusts and wild honey. And this was his message: "After me comes the one more powerful than I, the straps of whose sandals I am not worthy to stoop down and untie. I baptize you with water, but he will baptize you with the Holy Spirit." (Mark 1:4 – 8)

The "Holy Spirit" mentioned here by John the Baptist was an important part of the Old Testament promise concerning the future. The prophets declared that God's Spirit — which usually was powerfully present only in the work of kings and prophets — would be poured out "on all people" (Joel 2:28), giving them power to do God's will. Another prophet, Ezekiel, promised: "I will put my Spirit in you and move you to follow my decrees and be careful to keep my laws" (Ezekiel 36:27). The Baptist dipped people in water; he prepared people for the one who would drench people in the Spirit. More about this later.

JOHN THE BAPTIST IN HISTORY

We learn about John the Baptist's influence as a prophet not only from the gospel accounts, but also from non-Christian sources. Josephus, the first-century Jewish writer, refers to John the Baptist as an incredible prophet:

> But to some of the Jews the destruction of Herod's army seemed to be divine vengeance, and certainly a just vengeance, for his treatment of John, surnamed the Baptist. For Herod had put him to death, though he was a good man and had exhorted the Jews to lead righteous lives, to practise justice towards their fellows and piety towards God, and so doing to join in baptism. In his view this was a necessary preliminary if baptism was to be acceptable to God. They must not employ it to gain pardon for whatever sins they committed, but as a consecration of the body implying that the soul was already thoroughly cleansed by right behaviour. When others too joined the crowds about him, because they were aroused to the highest degree by his sermons, Herod became alarmed. Eloquence that had so great an effect on mankind might lead to some form of sedition, for it looked as if they would be guided by John in everything that they did. Herod decided therefore that it would be much better to strike first and be rid of him before his work led to an uprising, than to wait for an upheaval, get involved in a difficult situation and see his mistake. Though John, because of Herod's suspicions, was brought in chains to Machaerus, the stronghold that we have previously mentioned, and there put to death, yet the verdict of the Jews

was that the destruction visited upon Herod's army was a vindication of John, since God saw fit to inflict such a blow on Herod (Josephus, *Jewish Antiquities* 18.116–119).

THE ANOINTED ONE

Having described his account of Jesus as "gospel/good news" and claiming that John the Baptist was the great preparer foretold in the final lines of the Old Testament, Mark in his third paragraph introduces us to his main subject, a preacher from Galilee named Jesus. According to Mark (and the other gospel writers), the man from Nazareth cannot be included in the category "great teacher." For he is in fact the one the entire Old Testament has been waiting for. He is the king who surpasses David and will usher in the long-awaited kingdom of God. All of this and more is packed into some of the most significant lines in the New Testament. Let me quote them and then point out some of the more interesting elements of Mark's message about Jesus:

> At that time Jesus came from Nazareth in Galilee and was baptized by John in the Jordan. Just as Jesus was coming up out of the water, he saw heaven being torn open and the Spirit descending on him like a dove. And a voice came from heaven "You are my Son, whom I love; with you I am well pleased."
>
> At once the Spirit sent him out into the wilderness, and he was in the wilderness forty days, being tempted by Satan. He was with the wild animals, and angels attended him.
>
> After John was put in prison, Jesus went into Galilee,

proclaiming the good news [gospel] of God. "The time has come," he said. "The kingdom of God has come near. Repent and believe the good news!" (Mark 1:9–15).

Barrels of ink have been spent exploring the Old Testament resonances in these scenes. The number of PhDs written on this first chapter of Mark would surprise even the most technically minded lay reader. For instance, the scene of Jesus' baptism seems to function more like a *coronation* ceremony. As we saw in chapter 6, the Old Testament tells how the prophet Samuel was led to a young David. He secretly "anoints" the king and "from that day on," we are told in 1 Samuel 16:13, "the Spirit of the LORD came powerfully upon David." Here now at Jesus' baptism the prophet and preparer John the Baptist presides over an anointing and empowering from heaven. And just as Israelite kings were declared *metaphorically* to be "son of God," so Jesus receives this accolade from the heavens.

The connections run deeper. David's first acts as the "anointed one" were, as discussed in chapter 6, to expel the evil spirit from King Saul and destroy the evil Goliath. In the same way, the newly anointed Jesus contends with Satan himself in his desert experience and, by the power of God's Spirit, overcomes him. As strange as all the talk of "evil spirits" and "Satan" is to modern reader, there is no avoiding this dimension of the accounts of Jesus' life. Mark is falling over himself to record all the ways that Jesus is like ancient King David and yet, as the prophecies foretold, surpasses him. It hardly needs to be pointed out that one of the most consistent features of the Gospels' account of Jesus is his ministry of delivering people from evil and healing people from sickness. As Mark's narrative continues, story after story recounts Jesus exercising this "David-like" power:

> As soon as they left the synagogue, they went with James and John to the home of Simon and Andrew. Simon's mother-in-law was in bed with a fever, and they immediately told Jesus about her. So he went to her, took her hand and helped her up. The fever left her and she began to wait on them.
>
> That evening after sunset the people brought to Jesus all the sick and demon-possessed. The whole town gathered at the door, and Jesus healed many who had various diseases. He also drove out many demons, but he would not let the demons speak because they knew who he was. (Mark 1:29–34)

If this were another kind of book, I would outline the compelling reasons for concluding that Jesus — and, curiously, no other figure from ancient history — has exactly the kind of historical evidence you would expect a ministry of healing to leave behind and far more evidence pointing in that direction than you would expect if it were simply made up.

BOOK NOTES | No more comprehensive work has been written on the philosophical and historical credibility of Jesus' healing ministry than the two-volume work of the polymath Craig Keener, *Miracles: The Credibility of the New Testament Accounts* (Baker Academic, 2011).

My interest here, however, is the more literary or theological point that Jesus' encounter with "Satan" in the desert at the beginning of Mark and his power to heal and deliver people throughout the rest of the gospel underline his majesty as King David's greater son who is, in fact, the true and eternal Son of God.

NOW AND NOT YET

With all these Old Testament resonances in the air, Mark's opening chapter finally allows us to hear from the Messiah himself. And his message is brimming with expectation:

> Jesus went into Galilee proclaiming the good news of God. "The time has come," he said. "The kingdom of God has come near. Repent and believe the good news!" (Mark 1:14–15)

Everything about these words underlines how Jesus fulfills the hopes of the Old Testament. He proclaims "good news," the gospel that Isaiah predicted. The expression "the time has come" doesn't mean Jesus thinks it's about time to start a bit of healing and preaching. Literally, the words are "*fulfilled* is the time"! *The* time has arrived. All that the Old Testament promised about the reconciliation of mankind to God, the restoration of human communities, and the renewal of creation itself is about to come true.

In short, the "kingdom of God has come near," Jesus says. This is wonderful, but also a little anticlimactic. After all the energy and expectation built up thus far in Mark 1, we might have expected to read that the kingdom of God was *here,* not merely *near.* However, this is actually one of the key themes of the New Testament: in Jesus the kingdom of God is *inaugurated* but not yet brought to completion.

Some theologians refer to the New Testament perspective of the "now" and the "not yet." There is a tension built into the fabric of the New Testament between all that Christians have now because Christ's kingdom has come near and all that they will have when his kingdom fully comes. The ministry of Jesus recounted within the Gospels bears the marks of this now-but-not-yet motif. In some ways, wherever Jesus is present, speaking and healing, the future kingdom can be seen, heard, touched, and experienced. He is like the preview before the release of the blockbuster. But once Jesus departs the scene, Christians go on living here-and-now with only a kind of "deposit" of the future full payment of the kingdom or, to use another New Testament metaphor, the "firstfruits" of the full harvest yet to come (Romans 8:23; 1 Corinthians 15:20). As hard as this might be to get our heads around, it is basic to the broader teaching of the New Testament.

The kingdom of God has *begun,* and according to the New Testament, there are at least four things to show for it. First, in Jesus' death on the cross, Christians have forgiveness of sins right now. It is a point underlined time and time again in the Bible. Paul, for instance, declares that God has (and note the past and present tense verbs) "rescued us from the dominion of darkness and brought us into the kingdom of the Son he loves, in whom we have redemption, the forgiveness of sins" (Colossians 1:13 – 14). Again, the apostle John comforts us in the knowledge that "if we confess our sins, he [God] is faithful and just and will forgive us our sins" (1 John 1:9). The future tense verb here ("will forgive") does not refer to *when we get to heaven*; it means *at the time we confess our sins* to God.

This point cannot be emphasized strongly enough: the New Testament assures us that those who trust in Christ's death on our behalf enjoy God's forgiveness *now*, well in advance of the arrival of the kingdom and the day of judgment. Our future verdict can be known in the present, because all of our punishment has been laid on the Savior. That's what Jesus himself meant, in the passage quoted earlier, by saying that he came to "give his life as a ransom for many" (Mark 10:45). Without resting in this reality, there is little fruitful activity in the Christian life.

Second, because of Jesus' resurrection we can also have assurance of eternal life. As John's gospel quotes Jesus, "I am the resurrection and the life. The one who believes in me will live, even though they die; and whoever lives by believing in me will never die" (John 11:25 – 26). This dimension of the kingdom is ours now. As John later remarks in his first letter, "God has given us eternal life, and this life is in his Son. Whoever has the Son has life; whoever does not have the Son of God does not have life. I write these things to you who believe in the name of the Son of God so that you may know that you have eternal life" (1 John 5:11 – 13). What a privilege to know that you *have* eternal life!

BOOK NOTES

For those willing to read just one serious book on the historical evidence for the resurrection of Jesus, I recommend the eight-hundred-page tome by N. T. Wright, *The Resurrection of the Son of God* (Fortress, 2003). Tom Wright is a rarity in the world of scholarship. He has been both an ecclesiastical leader—as the former Anglican Bishop of Durham—and a widely recognized authority on the historical Jesus, now Research Professor of New Testament and Early Christianity at the University of St. Andrews, Scotland. The claim sometimes made that "Christian bias" disqualifies someone from writing seriously on historical matters concerning Jesus falls flat in the case of Wright, who never hides his Christian convictions but never relies on them as he engages in the most sophisticated kind of historical investigation.

Third, through Jesus' teachings we have a path to follow as we walk toward the goal of fully restored relationships (the social dimension of God's plan of redemption from Abraham to eternity). Chief here is his double commandment to love: "'Love the Lord your God with all your heart and with all your soul and with all your mind.' This is the first and greatest commandment. And the second is like it: 'Love your neighbor as yourself'" (Matthew 22:37–39). No doubt thinking of his Master's words, the apostle John put the point succinctly: "He has given us this command: Anyone who loves God must also love their brother and sister" (1 John 4:21). It is an obvious but endless reality of the Christian life: love reigns supreme. Despite bad press—not all of it undeserved — the church is a community of love. Christians naturally gather together to do Godward stuff (pray, sing, hear the Bible read and taught), but this is only half of what church is really about. God's "gathering" (which is what "church" means) is about serving each other's needs, sharing resources, meals, and lives with each other, and looking outward to the wider world to convey that same love through both practical care and (crucially) persuasion about the logic and beauty of Christ. I will say more about all this in the next chapter, but it can't be said too often that the church (in theory) is a place where love is obvious and overflowing, where the final social realities of God's kingdom are previewed.

Fourth, the future kingdom has broken into the present through the gift of the Holy Spirit to every believer. We saw earlier how John the Baptist heralded Jesus as the one prophesied about in the Old Testament, who would bring the power of God's Spirit. One of those ancient prophecies said that the Spirit would move God's people to "follow my [God's] decrees" (Ezekiel 11:20). In other words, the Spirit would enable us to put God's will into practice. This is why the apostle Paul can later speak of the Spirit's "fruit" in the life of the believer: "The fruit of the Spirit is love, joy, peace, forbearance, kindness, goodness, faithfulness, gentleness and self-control. Against such things there is no law" (Galatians 5:22 – 23).

In the next chapter, we will see that the Spirit also empowers God's people to stand up for Christ in public. For now I want to emphasize that the Holy Spirit is not some strange Force, as in the *Star Wars* movies, but the presence and power of God himself in the life of those who trust him. It is one of the blessings Christians enjoy *now* in anticipation of the future. Elsewhere in the New Testament the Holy Spirit is described as one of the "firstfruits" God has given us while we wait for full redemption (Romans 8:23) and as a "deposit guaranteeing our inheritance" (Ephesians 1:14). This language makes clear that Christians' experience of the Spirit now is only ever *partial*. It is a foretaste of the full life to come. They do not trouble themselves, therefore, if sometimes their best attempts at "love," "joy," "peace," and so on, feel like taking two steps forward and one step back (and some days two or three steps back). That's normal this side of the kingdom that Jesus will bring to completion.

There is plenty that Christians are still waiting for — the "not yet" part of existence. The New Testament is frank about that. They are looking forward to the final overthrow of evil that the Messiah will bring on his return. They hope for the end of pain and suffering, which the prophets said will come when the kingdom reigns. And they are waiting for the new creation of which the garden of Eden and Israel's Promised Land were previews. That's what the so-called second coming of Christ is all about. But more about that in the final chapter.

The kingdom of God is *near*, but it is not quite *here*. It is as if Jesus started the kingdom in his life, teaching, healings, death, resurrection, and gift of the Spirit, and then pressed the PAUSE button.

The "pause" is fabulous news. According to the New Testament, we currently live in a period of amnesty, when each of us can gladly welcome the King before the kingdom comes and overthrows all that is opposed to God's just and loving purposes. "The Lord is not slow in keeping his promise," said the apostle Peter to those wondering about the "pause." "Instead he is patient with you, not wanting anyone to perish, but everyone to come to repentance" (2 Peter 3:9). The kingdom is near but not fully here. That gives time for "repentance," says Peter — a word he heard from Jesus from the beginning of his preaching, as the opening paragraphs of Mark tell us.

CHANGED MIND

Jesus not only announced the kingdom; he urged people to respond to that reality. The word for that response in this opening chapter of the Gospel of Mark is "repent." "The kingdom of God has come near," Jesus declared. "Repent and believe the good news!" (Mark 1:15).

"Repent" has lost its luster in modern usage, but it is an important word in the Bible. In the original Greek of the New Testament, the verb "repent" is *metaneo*, which denotes a "change of mind." Jesus says that the appropriate response to the nearness of the kingdom of God is a *changed mind*. People should change their minds to *believe* that in Jesus the kingdom, the threefold restoration that the Old Testament looked forward to, has come. Trusting Jesus in this way — "trust" and "believe" are the same word in biblical Greek — is the core aspect of repentance, of the changed mind Jesus expected.

This is perhaps the place for a brief comment about the controversial word "faith." Richard Dawkins once wrote, "A case can be made that faith is one of the world's great evils, comparable to the smallpox virus but harder to eradicate. Faith, being belief that isn't based on evidence, is the principal vice of any religion" (*Daily Telegraph Science Extra*, September 11, 1989). However, in serious Christian literature "faith" is not used in the sense of believing things without reasons. That might be Richard Dawkins' preferred definition — except when he was publicly asked by Oxford professor John Lennox whether he had "faith" in his lovely wife — but it is important to know that in theology "faith" means personal trust in the God whose existence one already accepts on other grounds (whether philosophical, historical, experiential, or whatever).

Faith isn't about cognitively accepting the reality of God; it is about relying on, or trusting, him with our lives. It is more akin to the "trust" I have in my wife, which might not be based on logical or empirical "proof" but is grounded in good reasons. When Jesus called on people to repent and "believe/have faith" in the gospel, he was urging people to rely on its message, not think it was true (without reason).

BOOK NOTES | An informative and entertaining interaction with the "New Atheists" has been written by John Lennox, professor of mathematics at Oxford University: *Gunning for God: Why the New Atheists Are Missing the Target* (Lion, 2011).

Jesus says people are to change their minds to trust the gospel. So it is obvious what they are to change their minds *from*: from anything that keeps them from fully relying on his gospel. For some, I suspect, it is a proud fear that trusting Jesus will not cut the look of respectability in their particular social circle or that it will require them to take a different attitude to their money, relationships, work, sex life, and so on. For others, there is a preference for comfortable apathy, a contented sitting on the fence. For still others, it is an aversion to submitting to any lord, even one as credible and gracious as Jesus. To all of us, including the author of a book like this, Jesus says, "Repent and believe the good news!"

I gave a radio interview some years ago about one of my books. Australia's ABC *Triple J* is not renowned for a positive inclination toward Christianity, so I braced myself. It went surprisingly well. Toward the end of the hour they threw open the lines for callers. This was the moment I would be undone, I thought. Far from it. Everyone who called had favorable things to say about Jesus. They criticized the church, of course, but they seemed to love the man from Nazareth. "What a great teacher," one caller said. "What a great life coach," said another. It seemed that they viewed Jesus as a kind of Gandhi-figure writ large. Part of me was relieved that I emerged unscathed. Part of me was sad. As flattering as some of those views of Jesus are, they can also function as ways to contain him, to manage him. The Jesus they wanted was simply a good teacher, an ethical man, a guru. He was not the Jesus who announced the kingdom of God, who insisted that all God intended from the creation of the world was coming true in him, who demanded that people "repent."

Modifying Jesus to suit our preference is as common and easy as changing the TV channel. Don't like action drama?

Fine, switch to comedy. Don't like documentary? Easy, click sports. Disturbed by the thought that Jesus taught the truth, died for our sins, and rose again to establish the kingdom for eternity? Quick, give us the sweet baby Jesus or the lovely teacher of peace and love. It's a thought captured well by C. S. Lewis in a famous, if controversial, passage from the highly acclaimed *Mere Christianity*:

> A man who was merely a man and said the sort of things Jesus said would not be a great moral teacher. He would either be a lunatic—on the level with a man who says he is a poached egg—or else he would be the Devil of Hell. You must make your choice. You can shut Him up for a fool, you can spit at Him and kill Him as a demon; or you can fall at His feet and call Him Lord and God. But let us not come with any patronising nonsense about His being a great human teacher. He has not left that open to us. He did not intend to. (C. S. Lewis, *Mere Christianity* [HarperCollins, 1997], 43)

Some skeptics have criticized Lewis's reasoning here for leaving a gaping logical hole or two. Some contemporary theologians, fans of Lewis, have expressed similar reservations. Lewis forgets the other possibilities, they say. Perhaps Jesus wasn't a "liar," "lunatic," or "Lord"; maybe he did not actually say any of those grand things about himself—the gospel writers might have put it all on his lips decades later. Alternatively, perhaps Jesus was just mistaken about his identity. But it has to be remembered that Lewis's argument was made for those who retained a semblance of trust in the Gospels' reports about Jesus. He was just pointing out that if you happen to revere the Gospels and their portrait of Jesus, as many of his mid-twentieth-century readers did, then you don't really have the option to flatter him as a mere "great human teacher."

Lewis was certainly aware of more critical biblical scholars, who dismissed the Gospels as late inventions distorting the historical Jesus—he pokes fun at them in a brilliant essay titled "Fernseed and Elephants"—but in *Mere Christianity* he was not interested in such speculations. And as for the idea that Jesus was simply "mistaken" in imagining he was Lord of God's kingdom, I suspect Lewis would have equated that figure with "a man who says he is a poached egg." Thinking such things about yourself would not be a mistake but a certifiable delusion.

With a little qualification, Lewis's point remains. The figure in the Gospels cannot be reduced to a good moral teacher. Anything he says about morality is inextricably linked to his wider claim that his life, teaching, healings, death, and resurrection are what bring the kingdom near—and, one day, *here*.

ARCHAEOLOGY OF JESUS AS LORD AND GOD

It never ceases to surprise me how many people suspect that Jesus' status as divine, as "Lord and God," as Lewis puts it, was a much later invention. More precisely, people date it to the Council of Nicaea in the year AD 325. Emperor Constantine, so this story goes, wanted to elevate the simply human teacher Jesus to the status of a god, so that the empire could be united around a new deity pleasing to both Christians and pagans. He imposed this idea on church leaders, and so church folk ever since have assumed his divine status. This is the line given in Dan Brown's *The Da Vinci Code*, and many others have echoed its sentiment.

No one who knows the history of these matters gives this tale any credence, for the evidence that Christians worshiped Jesus as divine, pretty much from the beginning, is compelling. We have the words of the non-Christian Roman governor Pliny (AD 110). In a letter to Emperor Trajan inquiring as to whether he should keep killing Christians in his province (modern Turkey), he admits that he cannot really find just cause, for "the sum total of their guilt or error was no more than the following. They had met regularly before dawn on a determined day, and sung antiphonally [in alternate groups] a hymn to Christ as to a god" (Pliny, *Letters* 10.96). One such "hymn" to Christ as divine is preserved for us in the New Testament itself. In a letter of Paul to the Roman colony of Philippi (AD 60), the apostle breaks out into what (in Greek) is a clear rhyming rhythmic hymn declaring Jesus to be "in very nature God" (Philippians 2:6).

More striking than these literary examples of the worship of Jesus as divine is a recent archaeological discovery right in the middle of Israel. In a maximum security prison in Megiddo, workers in 2005 accidentally uncovered a mosaic floor that revealed a great house. As the dig continued, they discovered an entire ancient town, Kefar Othnay. The most important part of this find is a Christian prayer hall, perhaps an early form of a "church" building, which contains several wonderful mosaic inscriptions on the floor indicating its use by Christians. Of the seven named individuals in the inscriptions (other than Jesus) five are women.

One mosaic panel says, "Remember Primilla and Cyriaca and Dorothea, and moreover also Chreste." Perhaps these women were martyrs honored on the floor so everyone could recall their faith. Or perhaps they were benefactors or leaders of the church community. Either way, it underlines what scholars have often pointed out: women were key to the success of earliest Christianity.

The most dramatic of the inscriptions was commissioned by a woman named Akeptous. What she says about Jesus is powerful evidence, a century before Constantine and the Council of Nicaea, that churches revered Jesus as divine. The inscription is near a table structure, perhaps the table for Communion, and it reads: "The God-loving Akeptous has offered the table to God Jesus Christ as a memorial."

I have visited this site, which is still a prison, and as I stood on the mosaic floor, it was poignant to imagine that fellow believers met together in this very spot some 1,800 years earlier worshiping the same Lord. (Details of the excavation can be found in Yottam Tepper and Leah Di Segni, *A Christian Prayer Hall of the Third Century CE at Kefar Othnay (Legio): Excavations at the Megiddo Prison 2005* [Israel Antiquities Authority, 2006]).

Some serious scholars have developed detailed theories about how a first-century Palestinian Jewish teacher could so quickly be considered God-in-the-flesh. The important, if rather skeptical, scholar Bart Ehrman has given the question a fresh push recently in his book *How Jesus Became God: The Exaltation of a Jewish Preacher from Galilee* (Harper-One, 2014). Leading the discussion for the last decade or so, however, is Larry Hurtado of the University of Edinburgh. His *Lord Jesus Christ: Devotion to Jesus in Earliest Christianity* (Eerdmans, 2005) offers a highly sophisticated engagement with the complex historical evidence. It has little of the popular appeal of Ehrman's work, but rarely does the best scholarship attract wide media attention. A direct response to Ehrman's controversial claims by a number of [well-regarded specialists] can be found in Michael F. Bird, Craig F. Evans, Simon Gathercole, Charles E. Hill, Chris Tilling, *How God Became Jesus: The Real Origins of Belief in Jesus' Divine Nature—A Response to Bart D. Ehrman* [Zondervan, 2014].

FROM GALILEE TO THE WORLD

At the close of this chapter I will offer a selection of passages from the Gospels that give a taste of the breadth and depth of Jesus' teaching, deeds, death, and resurrection. I am conscious that slowing down as we have on the opening paragraphs of just one of the Gospels may obscure the forest for the trees. Yet I hope there is benefit in readers seeing that the New Testament's dependence on the Old Testament is not only massive, but it is expressed in subtle and sophisticated ways. You could spend your whole life studying the Bible and still not come close to plumbing the depths of the ways in which Jesus fulfills God's plans: "For no matter how many promises God has made," says the apostle Paul in the New Testament, "they are 'Yes' in Christ" (2 Corinthians 1:20).

There is one final dimension of Old Testament hope I want to explore before offering my Gospels "taster." It is an uncanny thought that the Lord of the world came out of Galilee. In his opening chapter, Mark casually indicates *where* Jesus' ministry started: "At that time Jesus came from Nazareth in Galilee and was baptized by John in the Jordan" (Mark 1:9); and again a few sentences later, "After John was put in prison, Jesus went into Galilee, proclaiming the good news of God" (Mark 1:14). Unlike Matthew, whose account of the same scenes draws deliberate attention to Jesus' *Galilean* origins, Mark does not appear to make anything of it — unless mentioning it twice is a subtle device. But the fact that Jesus was a Galilean — a point doubted by no serious historian today — resonates with one of the significant Old Testament predictions I mentioned in chapter 6. Isaiah 9 tells us that a "great light" would shine out of "Galilee," the boondocks of ancient Israel. The light, Isaiah says, is the "Prince of Peace," whose rule, as the promised descendent of King David, would know no end and no bounds. The Lord of the world would come out of Galilee.

I have no idea what could have nourished confidence in this prophecy in the centuries following Isaiah. Galilee was lovely and fertile, but it was not politically significant, and for much of its history it was populated in no small part by non-Jews or "Gentiles." Hope in such an ill-founded promise is another example of that Mandela-like prophetic madness I mentioned in chapter 7.

All the sources agree that Jesus grew up in Galilee and launched his ministry from there around the year AD 28. But only Matthew's gospel seems to spot the significance of this geo-historical quirk. Only he cites the prophecy of Isaiah 9 following his mention that Jesus began his ministry in

Galilee: "Galilee of the Gentiles — the people living in darkness have seen a great light," and so on (Matthew 4:12–16).

But even in Matthew's day, toward the end of the first century, there was not much observable evidence that the Christians' Galilean master was the universal Lord of Isaiah 9. Of course, what they had seen with their own eyes convinced them Isaiah's prophecy was sure to come true, but in the period in which they all lived, the evidence was squarely against the proposition that the message and rule of Jesus would know no end and no bounds.

The first three centuries of Christianity were marked by imperial oppression and persecution. Nothing in the early Christians' painful experience would have seemed like "proof" Jesus was on his way to conquering the heart of Rome, let alone capturing the allegiance of all the nations of the world. But they believed — with Mandela-like resolve against the evidence — and continued to preach and serve and die.

Their impossible dream came true. A Galilean has indeed changed the world and is worshiped today by more people in more countries than is any other figure. He is apparently also the most influential name in world history. Late in 2013 Cambridge University Press released *Who's Bigger? — Where Historical Figures Really Rank*, by Professors Steven Skiena and Charles Ward. The book aims to adjudicate on the debate over history's most influential people. It is no Christian book. It is a serious monograph tracking the historical, cultural, and ongoing international significance of thousands of people from Aristotle to Einstein and beyond, putting them through a mathematical model designed to reduce the subjective element in the authors' judgments, and then ranking the

historical figures. At the head of the list was Jesus of Nazareth, "an incredibly successful historical meme," said Skiena
in a recent interview with *Salon Magazine*. (It was a delightfully ironic description given that it was Richard Dawkins
who popularized the word "meme," a self-replicating social
idea, on the model of "gene").

A Galilean rules the world. How could this have been
stage-managed? A prophecy in 700 BC says the Lord of the
world would come out of lowly Galilee. Jesus came out of
Galilee—his life, death, and resurrection convinced his followers he is that Lord. Two thousand years later he is the most
revered and influential name in history. What are the odds
that a man from Galilee would become Lord of the world
and that there would be a prophecy several centuries earlier
predicting just that?

"CRIB NOTES" TO THE GOSPEL

As you read the Gospels, it is hard not to be taken by the
character of Jesus. He is stunning in his compassion, startling
in his strength, beautiful in his humility, and awe-inspiring
in his authority; he is utterly captivating. But the Gospels are
not simply biographies; they are accounts of biblical promises
fulfilled. Jesus is the Messiah who, through his life, teaching,
death, and resurrection, has come to save and restore. He is
the fulfillment of the Old Testament hopes and prophecies,
and he ushers in the great, beautiful, but also slightly terrifying, kingdom of God. This is what Christians have always
called "the gospel." This is why the first four books of the
New Testament—the ones that recount the life, death, and

resurrection of Jesus—have always been called the Gospels. It was reading these documents as a sixteen-year-old with no church background that first sparked my interest and, eventually, *trust* in Christianity.

To conclude this chapter I want to offer a series of readings from the Gospels, citing some of the key teachings and deeds of Jesus (along with a little commentary). In their different ways, these passages all speak of the way Jesus fulfills the spiritual, social, and physical dimensions of the kingdom first glimpsed in the garden of Eden and hoped for by ancient Israel. They provide a sort of "crib notes" to the Christian gospel.

How the Kingdom Calls for a Counter-Cultural Ethic

The so-called Sermon on the Mount contains some of the most famous teachings of Jesus. The "sermon" opens with a series of descriptions of those who will know the benefits of the coming kingdom of God. Steeped in Old Testament thought and language—too much to provide commentary here—this passage, known as the Beatitudes or Blessings, is a kind of manifesto of Jesus' vision of God's priorities in the world and in the future, and I love that it opens with a reassurance to those who know they have nothing to offer God.

Blessed are the poor in spirit, for theirs is the kingdom of heaven.
Blessed are those who mourn, for they will be comforted.
Blessed are the meek, for they will inherit the earth.
Blessed are those who hunger and thirst for righteousness, for they will be filled.

Blessed are the merciful, for they will be shown mercy.

Blessed are the pure in heart, for they will see God.

Blessed are the peacemakers, for they will be called children of God.

Blessed are those who are persecuted because of righteousness, for theirs is the kingdom of heaven.

(Matthew 5:3 – 10)

How Those Who Believe in the Kingdom Will Pray

Jesus despised showy prayers that conveyed one's piety. He called for simple, straightforward prayer to the one he called "Father." This is the so-called Lord's Prayer or Our Father. It may well be the most repeated religious statement in world history, being said in churches of all stripes throughout the Christian centuries. It is deceptively simple and gathers up all that Jesus wanted his followers to recall when they addressed the Almighty. This book is dedicated to the woman — my childhood baby-sitter — who taught me the words of the Lord's Prayer long before I knew anything else about Christianity.

> And when you pray, do not be like the hypocrites, for they love to pray standing in the synagogues and on the street corners to be seen by others. Truly I tell you, they have received their reward in full. But when you pray, go into your room, close the door and pray to your Father, who is unseen. Then your Father, who sees what is done in secret, will reward you. And when you pray, do not keep on babbling like pagans, for they think they will be heard because of their many words. Do not be

like them, for your Father knows what you need before you ask him.

This, then, is how you should pray:

Our Father in heaven,
hallowed be your name,
your kingdom come,
your will be done,
    on earth as it is in heaven.
Give us today our daily bread.
And forgive us our debts,
    as we also have forgiven our debtors.
And lead us not into temptation,
    but deliver us from the evil one. (Matthew 6:5–13)

(A traditional ending, appended to this prayer in some ancient manuscripts, reads: "For yours is the kingdom and the power and the glory forever. Amen." It is a fitting conclusion to such a majestic prayer.)

How the Kingdom Reverses the Power Paradigm of the World

One of the most common themes in the Gospels is the way God's kingdom upends expectations about authority, including divine authority. The majestic God is himself humbly breaking into the world and calling for our humility.

People were bringing little children to Jesus for him to place his hands on them, but the disciples rebuked them. When Jesus saw this, he was indignant. He said to them, "Let the little children come to me, and do not hinder them, for the kingdom of God belongs to such as these. Truly I tell you, anyone who will not receive the kingdom of God like a little child will never enter it."

And he took the children in his arms, placed his hands on them and blessed them. (Mark 10:13–16)

How Jesus' Healings and Powerful Deeds Provide a Glimpse, a Preview, of the Restoration of All Things

As odd as it may sound to modern ears, the Gospels portray Jesus' healing ministry not just as a demonstration of his power but as a public foreshadowing of what the kingdom, when it comes in full, will do for all creation: overthrow evil, restore sick bodies, bring life to the dead, and so on. In Jesus' miracles the kingdom arrived in miniature.

Then they brought him a demon-possessed man who was blind and mute, and Jesus healed him, so that he could both talk and see. All the people were astonished and said, "Could this be the Son of David?"

But when the Pharisees heard this, they said, "It is only by Beelzebul, the prince of demons, that this fellow drives out demons."

Jesus knew their thoughts and said to them, "Every kingdom divided against itself will be ruined, and every city or household divided against itself will not stand. If Satan drives out Satan, he is divided against himself. How then can his kingdom stand? And if I drive out demons by Beelzebul, by whom do your people drive them out? So then, they will be your judges. But if it is by the Spirit of God that I drive out demons, then the kingdom of God has come upon you." (Matthew 12:22–28)

How Becoming Right with God or "Justified" Is a Pure Gift of Divine Mercy

Some of what Jesus taught was directed against the religious presumption that moral and ritual performance merits God's favor and sets us apart from the "sinners" of the world. In the following parable — one of my favorites — Jesus contrasts God's view of a Pharisee (a member of a staunchly conservative religious faction of Jesus' day) and a tax collector (generally looked down upon as immoral and irreligious). The sting in the tail of the story is remarkable and should be pondered by everyone who wants to comprehend the uniqueness of Jesus.

> To some who were confident of their own righteousness and looked down on everyone else, Jesus told this parable: "Two men went up to the temple to pray, one a Pharisee and the other a tax collector. The Pharisee stood by himself and prayed: 'God, I thank you that I am not like other people — robbers, evildoers, adulterers — or even like this tax collector. I fast twice a week and give a tenth of all I get.'
>
> "But the tax collector stood at a distance. He would not even look up to heaven, but beat his breast and said, 'God, have mercy on me, a sinner.'
>
> "I tell you that this man, rather than the other, went home justified before God. For all those who exalt themselves will be humbled, and those who humble themselves will be exalted." (Luke 18:9–14)

How Jesus' Body and Blood Given on the Cross Fulfill the Ancient Passover Festival and the Promised "New Covenant"

In chapter 4, I explained that the premise of the law of Israel was God's great act of salvation in the exodus from Egypt. On the night of their deliverance itself, Israel was instructed to kill and eat a lamb and to place some of its blood on their doorposts. When God came in judgment on Egypt later that evening, he observed the sign of blood and passed over those Jewish households. Every year since then Jewish families have celebrated a Passover festival. In Jesus' day it involved buying a lamb, sacrificing it at the Jerusalem temple, and then taking it home to eat during the Seder or ceremonial Passover meal. The night before his crucifixion, Jesus ate a Seder in which he described his impending death as the ultimate Passover sacrifice that established the long-awaited "new covenant" of forgiveness of sins (also discussed in chapter 4).

> Then came the day of Unleavened Bread on which the Passover lamb had to be sacrificed. Jesus sent Peter and John, saying, "Go and make preparations for us to eat the Passover."
>
> "Where do you want us to prepare for it?" they asked.
>
> He replied, "As you enter the city, a man carrying a jar of water will meet you. Follow him to the house that he enters, and say to the owner of the house, 'The Teacher asks: Where is the guest room, where I may eat the Passover with my disciples?' He will show you a large room upstairs, all furnished. Make preparations there."
>
> They left and found things just as Jesus had told them. So they prepared the Passover.
>
> When the hour came, Jesus and his apostles reclined

at the table. And he said to them, "I have eagerly desired to eat this Passover with you before I suffer. For I tell you, I will not eat it again until it finds fulfillment in the kingdom of God.". . .

And he took bread, gave thanks and broke it, and gave it to them, saying, "This is my body given for you; do this in remembrance of me."

In the same way, after the supper he took the cup, saying, "This cup is the new covenant in my blood, which is poured out for you." (Luke 22:7–20)

How Jesus' Crucifixion Opens Up the Kingdom to the Sinner, Free of Charge

Just as in Jesus' ministry he handed out forgiveness to all who looked to him for mercy, so in the moments before his death on a cross he heard a criminal's plea for kindness and made an emphatic promise of welcome into God's kingdom. If you have ever doubted that Christianity offers salvation as a free gift, this passage surely inspires confidence and trust.

Two other men, both criminals, were also led out with him to be executed. When they came to the place called the Skull, they crucified him there, along with the criminals—one on his right, the other on his left. Jesus said, "Father, forgive them, for they do not know what they are doing." And they divided up his clothes by casting lots.

The people stood watching, and the rulers even sneered at him. They said, "He saved others; let him save himself if he is God's Messiah, the Chosen One."

The soldiers also came up and mocked him. They offered him wine vinegar and said, "If you are the king of the Jews, save yourself."

There was a written notice above him, which read: THIS IS THE KING OF THE JEWS.

One of the criminals who hung there hurled insults at him: "Aren't you the Messiah? Save yourself and us!"

But the other criminal rebuked him. "Don't you fear God," he said, "since you are under the same sentence? We are punished justly, for we are getting what our deeds deserve. But this man has done nothing wrong."

Then he said, "Jesus, remember me when you come into your kingdom."

Jesus answered him, "Truly I tell you, today you will be with me in paradise."

It was now about noon, and darkness came over the whole land until three in the afternoon, for the sun stopped shining. And the curtain of the temple was torn in two. Jesus called out with a loud voice, "Father, into your hands I commit my spirit." When he had said this, he breathed his last. (Luke 23:32–46)

How Jesus' Resurrection Establishes Israel's Hope for the Coming of the Kingdom

I said above that Jesus' healings were "previews" of the final kingdom, when God will restore all things. In a similar way, Jesus' resurrection is not just a display of power or a way of marking his credentials. It is the first great act of new life in God's kingdom. The man who arranged the burial of Jesus is described as "waiting for the kingdom of God." While he didn't know it yet, his hopes would come to fruition a couple of days later with the resurrection of Jesus. The death of the Messiah was not the end of his proclaimed kingdom; rather, through the resurrection it was a doorway to the future. The resurrection of Jesus is God's pledge within history that he can and will restore all things at the climax of history.

> Joseph of Arimathea, a prominent member of the Council, who was himself waiting for the kingdom of God, went boldly to Pilate and asked for Jesus' body.... So Joseph bought some linen cloth, took down the body, wrapped it in the linen, and placed it in a tomb cut out of rock. Then he rolled a stone against the entrance of the tomb. Mary Magdalene and Mary the mother of Joseph saw where he was laid.
>
> When the Sabbath was over, Mary Magdalene, Mary the mother of James, and Salome bought spices so that they might go to anoint Jesus' body....
>
> But when they looked up, they saw that the stone, which was very large, had been rolled away. As they entered the tomb, they saw a young man dressed in a white robe sitting on the right side, and they were alarmed.
>
> "Don't be alarmed," he said. "You are looking for Jesus the Nazarene, who was crucified. He has risen! He is not here. See the place where they laid him. But go, tell his disciples and Peter, 'He is going ahead of you into Galilee. There you will see him, just as he told you.'" (Mark 15:43 – 16:7)

How the Entire Story of Jesus, Climaxing in His Death and Resurrection, Fulfills the Old Testament

In the resurrection account of Luke's gospel, Jesus explains to the stunned disciples that his life, death, and resurrection for the forgiveness of the world are what the whole Old Testament — described here as "the Law of Moses, the Prophets and the Psalms" — is about.

While they were still talking about this, Jesus himself stood among them and said to them, "Peace be with you."

They were startled and frightened, thinking they saw a ghost. He said to them, "Why are you troubled, and why do doubts rise in your minds? Look at my hands and my feet. It is I myself! Touch me and see; a ghost does not have flesh and bones, as you see I have."

When he had said this, he showed them his hands and feet. And while they still did not believe it because of joy and amazement, he asked them, "Do you have anything here to eat?" They gave him a piece of broiled fish, and he took it and ate it in their presence.

He said to them, "This is what I told you while I was still with you: Everything must be fulfilled that is written about me in the Law of Moses, the Prophets and the Psalms."

Then he opened their minds so they could understand the Scriptures. He told them, "This is what is written: The Messiah will suffer and rise from the dead on the third day, and repentance for the forgiveness of sins will be preached in his name to all nations, beginning at Jerusalem. (Luke 24:36–47)

In Jesus' teaching he described what it means to live now for the coming kingdom. In his deeds of healing he provided a glimpse of the kingdom and the restoration it would bring. Ultimately, through his death and resurrection he bears the judgment humanity deserves so that even the most undeserving may freely enter the kingdom. As Jesus indicated in his opening statement as recorded in the Gospel of Mark, the kingdom might not be here quite yet, but it is well and truly "near." Christians try to live in the light of all this.

THROUGH THE MISSION OF THE CHURCH OF THE FIRST CENTURY

The next book in the New Testament after the Gospels is the book of the Acts of the Apostles, or Acts for short. It is the only book in the New Testament, apart from the Gospels, to contain narrative recounts of events rather than letters of instruction or prophecy. It details what the followers of Jesus did after Jesus died, rose to life, and ascended (that is, left the earth to go back to the Father). It was written by Luke, the man who wrote the gospel of the same name, and Acts functions as a second volume continuing on from his gospel with the account of the spread of the message about Jesus.

Through the Mission of the Church to the End of the First Century

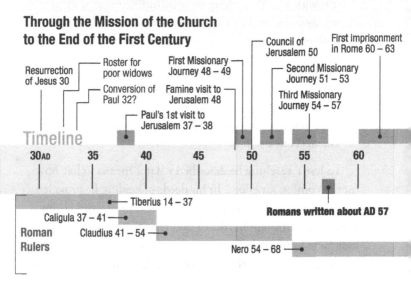

Resurrection of Jesus 30

Roster for poor widows

Conversion of Paul 32?

Paul's 1st visit to Jerusalem 37 – 38

First Missionary Journey 48 – 49

Famine visit to Jerusalem 48

Council of Jerusalem 50

First imprisonment in Rome 60 – 63

Second Missionary Journey 51 – 53

Third Missionary Journey 54 – 57

Timeline

30 AD 35 40 45 50 55 60

Tiberius 14 – 37

Caligula 37 – 41

Romans written about AD 57

Roman Rulers

Claudius 41 – 54

Nero 54 – 68

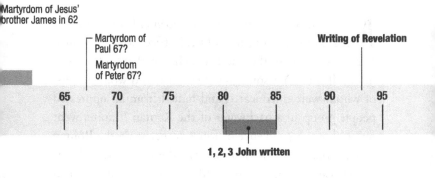

Martyrdom of Jesus'
brother James in 62

Martyrdom of
Paul 67?

Martyrdom
of Peter 67?

Writing of Revelation

| 65 | 70 | 75 | 80 | 85 | 90 | 95 |

1, 2, 3 John written

Vespasian 69 – 79

Titus 79 – 81

Domitian 81 – 96

9

THE GREAT WORK: THE "CHURCH" AFTER JESUS

YOU WILL BE MY WITNESSES IN JERUSALEM, AND IN ALL JUDEA AND SAMARIA, AND TO THE ENDS OF THE EARTH.

(ACTS 1:8)

At the time of his death, Jesus, a carpenter from Nazareth, with no money and no political office, who was killed after three years in the public eye, had perhaps a few hundred followers. Yet somehow these men and women, most of whom were uneducated and hailed from an oppressed people group in a backwater of the Roman Empire, went on, without any violence or force, to persuade the Roman Empire that the crucified one was the true Lord. This is simply astounding—some would say miraculous. My own doctoral research focused on the background and extent of the early Christian mission, and I remain genuinely baffled by its zeal and success.

The topic of Christian mission is a fraught one, with its own boo-words: "evangelism" or, worse, "proselytizing." It may surprise readers to know that even long-term Christians sometimes feel uncomfortable with the idea of "spreading the word." I was once caught out myself. I was confronted in a café by a woman who overheard the conversation I was having with a fellow clergyman about how my church was seeking to promote Christ to our local area. She strode up to my table and, at what seemed like the top of her voice, in front of numerous other customers (my neighbors), she declared, "So, you want to convert the world. How dare you!" I had no reply, witty or otherwise (until long after she'd gone), and for a moment I wondered about the reasonableness of the ancient Christian practice of seeking "converts."

There was a humorous Christian book, a minor classic published in the early 1990s, called *The Sacred Diary of Adrian Plass*. It is the fictional journal of a very ordinary English Christian. In the imaginary entry for Sunday January 12, he articulates beautifully the ambivalence many feel about "evangelism":

> Sermon on witnessing by Reverend Edwin. Very good. Made you want to go straight out and witness to somebody. Drifted off into a pleasant daydream in which I began to preach in the street and ended up with a huge crowd of people all repenting in tears and being healed of their sickness just by the touch of my hand. I was very near tears myself during the hymn that followed as I pictured myself addressing vast assemblies of needy people throughout the world. I came to with a shock as I realized that Reverend Edwin was asking for people to volunteer to do some actual street evangelism next Friday.

> Sat down as low in my seat as I possibly could trying to
> look like someone whose earnest desire to evangelise had
> been thwarted by a previous appointment. (Adrian Plass,
> *The Sacred Diary of Adrian Plass* [Zondervan, 1993], 22)

Though "witnessing" and "evangelizing" represent a
source of awkwardness for some believers, and scorn from
skeptics, it is worth noting that sharing the good news
of Christ is not some irritating, guilt-inducing pastime
invented by a few overly zealous believers. It is the very *mission* of the church, given to it by none other than Jesus.

ACT 1 OF THE APOSTLES

After his life, teaching, death, and resurrection, Jesus
gave his followers a task. It is a task—a mission—that is
described in the book of Acts. The twenty-five-year history
of the first church recounted in Acts begins, as its foundation, with the command of the risen Christ to "be my
witnesses in Jerusalem, and in all Judea and Samaria, and
to the ends of the earth" (Acts 1:8). Because of its significance, the opening lines of Acts deserve to be quoted in full.
The fact that you are reading this book, two thousand years
after Jesus, on the other side of the world, is proof that what
began in this passage has had the most extraordinary influence on the world:

> In my former book, Theophilus, I wrote about all that
> Jesus began to do and to teach until the day he was taken
> up to heaven, after giving instructions through the Holy
> Spirit to the apostles he had chosen. After his suffering,
> he presented himself to them and gave many convincing

proofs that he was alive. He appeared to them over a period of forty days and spoke about the kingdom of God. On one occasion, while he was eating with them, he gave them this command: "Do not leave Jerusalem, but wait for the gift my Father promised, which you have heard me speak about. For John baptized with water, but in a few days you will be baptized with the Holy Spirit."

Then they gathered around him and asked him, "Lord, are you at this time going to restore the kingdom to Israel?"

He said to them: "It is not for you to know the times or dates the Father has set by his own authority. But you will receive power when the Holy Spirit comes on you; and you will be my witnesses in Jerusalem, and in all Judea and Samaria, and to the ends of the earth."

After he said this, he was taken up before their very eyes, and a cloud hid him from their sight.

They were looking intently up into the sky as he was going, when suddenly two men dressed in white stood beside them. "Men of Galilee," they said, "why do you stand here looking into the sky? This same Jesus, who has been taken from you into heaven, will come back in the same way you have seen him go into heaven." (Acts 1:1–11)

Given the high expectations Jesus created with statements like, "The time has come.... The kingdom of God has come near" (Mark 1:15), it is understandable that following his resurrection, the disciples would wonder if the kingdom would now fully "appear," not just remain "near." Hence the question Luke says the disciples asked: "Lord, are you at this time going to restore the kingdom to Israel?" (Acts 1:6). Instead of answering the question, Jesus gives his followers a task—to take the news about the kingdom to every nation, to "the ends of the earth." Eighteen hundred years earlier, the great patriarch Abraham had been told, "all peoples on earth will be blessed through you." Now a descendant of Abraham, from the line of King David, sends out that worldwide blessing in the form of a message, an invitation to all people everywhere to enter God's kingdom.

I have said before that Jesus brought the kingdom close enough to touch and then pressed PAUSE. This is great news, as I also indicated, for it means there is a period of amnesty, a time to receive Christ gladly before his kingdom overthrows all that is opposed to his good purposes. More than that, this "pause" gives those who have tasted the good things of the kingdom a chance to pass them on to others before the end of the amnesty. Instead of answering the question of when the kingdom will be fulfilled, Jesus gives his followers the task of spreading its benefits. It is not too much to say that the very reason for the hiatus between the nearness of the kingdom and the final appearance of the kingdom is the evangelistic mission of the church.

According to the passage just quoted, the believers seem to have imagined that the gift of the Holy Spirit, prophesied by the Old Testament prophets, promised by John the Baptist, and reiterated now by Jesus, was the sign that the kingdom was about to be wrapped up. It was a fair assumption for those who read their Old Testaments. The prophets Isaiah, Ezekiel, and Joel had all associated the outpouring of God's Spirit with the fulfillment of his plans for the world: "I will pour water on the thirsty land, and streams on the dry ground," Isaiah declared on God's behalf centuries earlier; "I will pour out my Spirit on your offspring, and my blessing on your descendants" (Isaiah 44:3). According to Jesus, however, the gift of the Spirit means there's work to do in the world: "you will receive power when the Holy Spirit comes on you; and you will be my witnesses in Jerusalem" (Acts 1:8). The gift of the Holy Spirit is not the culmination of the kingdom; rather, it is the power the church needs to send the invitation of the kingdom out to all the nations. This is the real explanation of the miraculous success of the church's mission (in the history department of a secular university, however, this was not a line of enquiry open to me in my research).

The rest of the book of Acts records the first twenty-five or so years of the Christian mission, as the apostles and others bear witness to Jesus: in Jerusalem and Judea in chapters 2–7, Samaria in chapter 8, and, following the conversion of the persecutor-turned-missionary Saul/Paul in chapter 9, to the full spectrum of the Greco-Roman world, including Caesarea, Cyprus, Syria, Turkey, and Greece, via the momentous decision of the Jerusalem leaders in chapter 15 to admit all these Gentiles to Christian faith *without the Jewish sign of circumcision.* In the final chapters of Acts, the message reaches the capital itself. In the closing lines, after twenty-eight rollicking chapters, we find the apostle Paul in Rome, under house arrest, awaiting trial, but continuing his mission:

> For two whole years Paul stayed there in his own rented house and welcomed all who came to see him. He proclaimed the kingdom of God and taught about the Lord Jesus Christ — with all boldness and without hindrance! (Acts 28:30–31)

This paragraph is a marvelous conclusion to the earliest recorded history of the church. Whether intended or not, Luke strikes the twin themes of the church's story throughout the best moments of its history: the willing renunciation of earthly privilege and power (Paul is at the mercy of the Roman court) combined with a happy reliance on *mere persuasion* to advance Christ's cause. The modern church, especially in the West, would do well to remember this winning combination. Christ does not require political, legal, or military power to achieve his purposes. He simply asks for a people willing to suffer and persuade (in the power of the Spirit). Croatian-born theologian Miroslav Volf, now a professor at Yale University, was recently on national television in Australia, where he was asked about "media persecution" of Christians in the West. His response was powerful and intriguing:

> I grew up in a society that was radically secular, that was completely in the domination of the Communist Party and the whole media, education, and government was shaped from that perspective. To be a Christian was to be a second, third class citizen. You know, I don't think it did me harm. I think it's a good thing,... Church was born as a marginal institution. For many centuries it stayed as a marginal institution, and I think if we are detached from power, we can see things much more clearly; we can project authentic Christian vision much more—much better. I think it's healthy for the church to learn how to live from the margins and contribute from the margins to the well-being of society. (ABC, *Q&A*, March 17, 2014)

It is one of the true puzzles of history that a small Jewish movement won over the Roman Empire without weapons. I cannot tell you how many historians have poured out their intellect and written volume after volume trying to explain the unthinkable: conquering an empire with little more than words and acts of kindness. But this is exactly what the Bible promised in its first book. Abraham was told that he would become a great nation and that, as a result, he would bring blessing to *all* nations. After Jesus' ascension, a little band of Israelites, descendants of Abraham, was sent out to the ends of the earth with news of this blessing. And the unthinkable happened. If only father Abraham could see what he started!

Of course, not every Christian is called to be a missionary in the sense we find in the book of Acts. It is called the "Acts *of the Apostles*" for a reason. The average believer through Christian history never imagined that they bore the same mission responsibility as those original witnesses and those who succeeded them. The wider teaching of the New Testament emphasizes how ordinary Christians *promote* the gospel that evangelists *proclaim*. They do this by living lives of love that draw people to Christ (Matthew 5:14–16), by praying for the ongoing success of the mission (Ephesians 6:19–20; 2 Thessalonians 3:1), and by being prepared to "give an answer" for the faith whenever opportunity allows (Colossians 4:5–6; 1 Peter 3:13–15).

BOOK NOTES

A few years ago, I wrote a book that tries to unpack the total teaching of the Bible about how "ordinary Christians," through their daily lives, can promote the Christian faith to the wider world: *The Best Kept Secret of Christian Mission: Promoting the Gospel with More Than Our Lips* (Zondervan, 2010). The

BOOK
NOTES

overblown title is not meant to convey the importance of my
book (!) but simply to point out that contemporary Christians
sometimes miss the liberating thing the Bible asks them to do
for the cause of Christ: not become "evangelists" but rather
humble "promoters" of Christ as their personality, circumstances, gifts, and opportunities allow.

WHAT ABOUT SOCIAL JUSTICE?

It is worth pausing to reflect briefly on a contemporary
question that is sometimes raised as Christians struggle to
work out the church's priorities in the world.

There is confusion over whether the church's core mission is to *care for the poor* or to *preach the gospel*. Some
churches emphasize social action, while others emphasize
the proclamation of the message. Many churches attempt
a hybrid of the two, as if the mission of Jesus is twofold,
preaching the truth and serving the needy. I feel the debate
confuses categories; it mistakes what the church *is*, with the
task Christ has given it. It blurs the church's *character* with
its *mission*. Let me explain.

There is no doubt the church of Christ is meant to be
a community shaped by God's love. Loving the poor and
vulnerable is its constitution, its DNA. A church therefore
that does not care for the needy isn't defying its "mission" as
such. It is worse. It is defying its essence, its very self. That
said, to this church, constituted by love, Christ has given a
mission—to take the good news of the kingdom to all the
world. There is no avoiding the centrality of *communicating*

the gospel in the book of Acts, the main source of our knowledge of what the first Christians saw as their mission. Jesus did not give his church two competing missions. He gave it one mission: to spread the gospel. Yet, this church is not the true church unless it is meeting the needs of the poor wherever it finds them. Only a church whose DNA is to care for the needy is fit for the mission of taking Christ's gospel to the world.

We find this combination of ideas in the book of Acts itself. Early on in the life of the church, it became clear that the needs of the poor were so great that they could potentially distract the apostles from the task of preaching. Instead of sidelining social care, they dedicated a group of individuals charged with ensuring that the human needs were being met, so that the designated witnesses to Jesus could focus on being witnesses:

> In those days when the number of disciples was increasing, the Hellenistic Jews among them complained against the Hebraic Jews because their widows were being overlooked in the daily distribution of food. So the Twelve gathered all the disciples together and said, "It would not be right for us to neglect the ministry of the word of God in order to wait on tables. Brothers and sisters, choose seven men from among you who are known to be full of the Spirit and wisdom. We will turn this responsibility over to them and will give our attention to prayer and the ministry of the word."
>
> This proposal pleased the whole group. They chose Stephen, a man full of faith and of the Holy Spirit; also Philip, Procorus, Nicanor, Timon, Parmenas, and Nicolas from

Antioch, a convert to Judaism. They presented these men to the apostles, who prayed and laid their hands on them.

So the word of God spread. The number of disciples in Jerusalem increased rapidly, and a large number of priests became obedient to the faith. (Acts 6:1–7)

This task of caring for the needy, and doing so through an order of ministers known as "deacons," became a huge part of the ministry of the church, right up to today. By AD 250 the church of Rome, still a community under threat of persecution, had no fewer than fourteen deacons in service. The church was supporting the daily needs of "fifteen hundred widows and persons in distress" (Eusebius, *Ecclesiastical History* 6.43.11).

Even tiny churches did what they could to meet the needs of the poor around them. In an account of legal proceedings from half a century later (during the most severe persecution of Christians in Roman history) we learn about the church of Cirta, North Africa. Officials in this period sought to loot and destroy Christian buildings, books, and "treasures." The list of goodies found in the basement of the church of Cirta provides an insight into the DNA of ancient Christianity: 16 tunics for men, 82 dresses for women, 13 pairs of men's shoes, 47 pairs of women's shoes, 19 peasant capes, 10 vats of oil and wine. Officials had stumbled across the true treasure of this church—its storage room for the local poor (Apatus, *Proceedings before Zenophilus* 3–4).

While muted by despicable scandals sweeping the modern church, it remains the case today that churches never turn their back on the needs of the poor. My own denomination, the Church of England (Anglican or Episcopalian), still ordains men and women to the Order of Deacon, "to search for the sick, poor, and impotent people of the Parish, that they may be relieved with the alms of the Parishioners" (*Book of Common Prayer*). To this day, eighteen of the twenty-four largest charities by revenue in Australia are *Christian*.

Today, as in the first century, involvement in the church always entails a commitment to both its evangelistic mission and its compassionate essence, its raison d'être and modus operandi.

I am pleased to say that this is something the church in Australia got right at the founding of our colony (despite its numerous mistakes since). On January 26, 1788, the Rev. Mr. Richard Johnson stepped off the First Fleet onto Australian soil as Chaplain to the Colony of New South Wales. A Cambridge-trained Anglican priest of the evangelical wing of the church, Johnson was a friend of the former slave-trader and convert John Newton (of "Amazing Grace" fame) and the great anti-slavery campaigner William Wilberforce. Johnson had none of the charisma or impact of these eighteenth-century giants, but, like them, he saw no tension between his priestly duties of preaching, leading church services, and marrying and burying, and the equally pressing duties of serving the good of our young colony. Well known is his struggle with the leadership of the colony to construct a church. When he eventually built it (out of his own funds), it was burnt to the ground in suspicious circumstances. Some see this as a parable of Australian resistance to the church! Less well known today is Johnson's fame in the 1790s as the best farmer in the colony, a skill he shared with others—to the benefit of everyone. He also engaged with convicts and officers alike and refused to play the role of "moral police-man," as successive governors had hoped. He sought to convey peace even to the most irreligious and immoral.

Johnson was also committed to peace with the indigenous peoples, strongly supporting the policy of building genuine friendships. He adopted an indigenous orphan into his family, and later gave his own daughter the Aboriginal name, Milbah. On one occasion he even offered himself as human "collateral," remaining hostage with a local tribe while the great Aboriginal chief Benelong met with Governor Arthur Philip.

Perhaps most impressive is Johnson's tireless efforts with the sick and dying. Against (all good) advice, he visited the diseased and putrid holds of ships where convicts lay listless and abandoned. One convict wrote home, amid the sickness and hunger of 1790, mentioning Johnson by name: "few of the sick would recover if it was not for the kindness of the Rev. Mr. Johnson, whose assistance out of his own stores makes him the physician both of soul and body" (taken from the official entry in the *Australian Dictionary of Biography*, Australia's preeminent dictionary of national biography, available online at http.adb.anu.edu.au). It's not a bad image of the church's mission and character as revealed in the book of Acts: to be "physician both of soul and body."

The "soul-work" of Johnson is also noteworthy. His first sermon on the Sunday following disembarkation was to the nine hundred convicts and marines that made up the colony, assembled under a great tree by Sydney Harbour. He chose Psalm 116:12 as his text: "What shall I render unto the Lord for all his benefits toward me?" He was not a moralist but a herald of the goodness—the "benefits"—of the Creator toward all, including criminals.

Perhaps the most stunning example of Johnson's work comes from six months later. Samuel Peyton was a young petty thief given "seven years transportation" for stealing a watch in London. Within a few months of arriving at Sydney Cove, he was caught in an officer's quarters trying to steal "a shirt, stockings and a comb." Peyton was promptly tried and sentenced on Monday, June 23, 1788, and on the Wednesday following he was hanged on Sydney's public gallows (where a five-star hotel now stands). He was just twenty-one years old. Peyton would be just another name in a convict log were it not for a letter he wrote to his mother with the assistance of an unnamed friend the night before his hanging (we have a copy of the letter). It was the Rev. Richard Johnson's duty to visit the condemned. Given the highly evangelical Anglican character of the letter's theology and language, it seems plausible, if not likely, that Johnson was the one to help this young man face eternity trusting in the gospel of Jesus Christ—and wanting to tell his mother so. The letter reads in part:

My dear mother,

With what agony of soul do I dedicate the few last moments of my life to bid you an eternal adieu: my doom being irrevocably fixed, and ere this hour tomorrow I shall have entered into an unknown and endless eternity. Too late I regret my inattention to your admonitions, and feel myself sensibly affected by the remembrance of the many anxious moments you have passed on my account. For these and all my other transgressions, however great, I supplicate the Divine forgiveness; and encouraged by the promises of that Saviour who died for us all, I trust to receive that mercy in the world to come, which my offences have deprived me of in this. Sincerely penitent for my sins; sensible of the justice of my conviction and sentence, and firmly relying on the merits of a Blessed Redeemer, I trust I shall yet experience that peace which this world cannot give.

Your unhappy dying son,

Samuel Peyton,
Sydney Cove, Port Jackson,
New South Wales, 24th June 1788

Richard Johnson's work as "physician both of soul and body" is, for me, a lovely example of the church's *mission* and *character* throughout history. In their best moments, believers try to make known the message of Christ's death and resurrection — some working as "evangelists," most as humble "promoters." But, equally, they help those in need wherever they find them. They launch programs for widows, visit the sick and dying, establish charities, and strive to be good neighbors. In short, however incompletely they manage to pull it off, the church promotes and embodies the gospel. For all the failures of church history, this is the true heritage of those first "witnesses" in the book of Acts.

BOOK NOTES   In the late 1990s, sociology professor Rodney Stark wrote an excellent little book on the missionary growth of the early Christians, *The Rise of Christianity: How the Obscure, Marginal Jesus Movement Became the Dominant Religious Force*

---

in the Western World in a Few Centuries (HarperSanFransisco, 1997). He picks up where the book of Acts leaves off and takes us through the next few hundred years. He writes, he tells us, as a non-Christian. Yet, he is extremely positive about the social benefits of early Christian preaching and care. I don't agree with everything in the book: on the one hand, he is overly skeptical about the numerical growth described in the book of Acts; and, on the other hand, he is probably overly optimistic about the number of confessing Christians in the empire by AD 350 (up to half the population, he reckons). Still, his approach and conclusions are exciting and informative, and, unlike much written on the topic, its style is accessible.

"CRIB NOTES" TO THE APOSTLES' TEACHING

The book of Acts documents the rapid and remarkable spread of Christianity throughout the Mediterranean as the apostles and others preached the gospel of God's kingdom (and cared for those in need). But as this message spread, so too did confusion about doctrine and how to live in the light of the message that people had received. Most of the rest of the New Testament—the next twenty-two books—are letters written by the first generation of Christian leaders to church communities or individuals explaining various parts of Christian theology and practice.

These books are called "epistles," which simply means "letters," and many of them were written by characters we meet in the Gospels and Acts, such as Peter, John, James, and Paul. In what follows I want to give you a taste of the teachings of these writers who, in the midst of the kind of mission busyness we observe in the book of Acts, wrote to fledgling Christian communities to strengthen their faith, hope, and love. These texts remain a source of immense intellectual and practical stimulation in the twenty-first century. Christians revere these letters, just as they revere the words of Jesus, as God's Word. After all, they were written by Christ's "ambassadors."

A Rich Passage from Paul's Letters

Here is a dense but rich passage from Paul (who wrote thirteen letters in the New Testament) about how Christ's death "atones" for our wrongdoing and "justifies" us (makes us right) in God's eyes:

> Now we know that whatever the law says, it says to those who are under the law, so that every mouth may be silenced and the whole world held accountable to God. Therefore no one will be declared righteous in God's sight by the works of the law; rather, through the law we become conscious of our sin.
>
> But now apart from the law the righteousness of God has been made known, to which the Law and the Prophets testify. This righteousness is given through faith in Jesus Christ to all who believe. There is no difference between Jew and Gentile, for all have sinned and fall short of the glory of God, and all are justified freely by his grace through the redemption that came by Christ Jesus. God presented Christ as a sacrifice of atonement, through the shedding of his blood — to be received by faith. He

did this to demonstrate his righteousness, because in his forbearance he had left the sins committed beforehand unpunished—he did it to demonstrate his righteousness at the present time, so as to be just and the one who justifies those who have faith in Jesus. (Romans 3:19–26)

Paul's Summary of the Christian Life

Here is Paul's summary of the Christian life as "worship" flowing from God's mercy—covering ministry in church, relationships with other Christians, and service in society:

Therefore, I urge you, brothers and sisters, in view of God's mercy, to offer your bodies as a living sacrifice, holy and pleasing to God—this is your true and proper worship. Do not conform to the pattern of this world, but be transformed by the renewing of your mind. Then you will be able to test and approve what God's will is—his good, pleasing and perfect will.

For by the grace given me I say to every one of you: Do not think of yourself more highly than you ought, but rather think of yourself with sober judgment, in accordance with the faith God has distributed to each of you. For just as each of us has one body with many members, and these members do not all have the same function, so in Christ we, though many, form one body, and each member belongs to all the others. We have different gifts, according to the grace given to each of us. If your gift is prophesying, then prophesy in accordance with your faith; if it is serving, then serve; if it is teaching, then teach; if it is to encourage, then give encouragement; if it is giving, then give generously; if it is to lead, do it diligently; if it is to show mercy, do it cheerfully.

Love must be sincere. Hate what is evil; cling to what is good. Be devoted to one another in love. Honor one another above yourselves. Never be lacking in zeal, but keep your spiritual fervor, serving the Lord. Be joyful in hope, patient in affliction, faithful in prayer. Share with the Lord's people who are in need. Practice hospitality.

Bless those who persecute you; bless and do not curse. Rejoice with those who rejoice; mourn with those who mourn. Live in harmony with one another. Do not be proud, but be willing to associate with people of low position. Do not be conceited.

Do not repay anyone evil for evil. Be careful to do what is right in the eyes of everyone. If it is possible, as far as it depends on you, live at peace with everyone. (Romans 12:1 – 18)

Paul's Famous Reflection on Christian Love

Love is patient, love is kind. It does not envy, it does not boast, it is not proud. It does not dishonor others, it is not self-seeking, it is not easily angered, it keeps no record of wrongs. Love does not delight in evil but rejoices with the truth. It always protects, always trusts, always hopes, always perseveres.

Love never fails. But where there are prophecies, they will cease; where there are tongues, they will be stilled; where there is knowledge, it will pass away. For we know in part and we prophesy in part, but when completeness comes, what is in part disappears. When I was a child, I talked like a child, I thought like a child, I reasoned like a child. When I became a man, I put the ways of childhood behind me. For now we see only a reflection as in a

mirror; then we shall see face to face. Now I know in part;
then I shall know fully, even as I am fully known.

And now these three remain: faith, hope and love.
But the greatest of these is love. (1 Corinthians 13:4–13)

Paul's Call to Humility

Paul calls believers to a life of humility based on the humility of Christ (here the apostle cites what may be the earliest
Christian "hymn"):

Do nothing out of selfish ambition or vain conceit. Rather,
in humility value others above yourselves, not looking to
your own interests but each of you to the interests of the
others.

In your relationships with one another, have the same
mindset as Christ Jesus:

Who, being in very nature God,
  did not consider equality with God something to
    be used to his own advantage;
rather, he made himself nothing
  by taking the very nature of a servant,
  being made in human likeness.
And being found in appearance as a man,
  he humbled himself
  by becoming obedient to death —
    even death on a cross!
Therefore God exalted him to the highest place
  and gave him the name that is above every name,
that at the name of Jesus every knee should bow
  in heaven and on earth and under the earth,
and every tongue acknowledge that Jesus Christ is Lord,
  to the glory of God the Father. (Philippians 2:3–11)

A Mission Message to Timothy

Paul emphasizes to his missionary apprentice Timothy the importance of continuing the mission of preaching Christ to all:

> In the presence of God and of Christ Jesus, who will judge the living and the dead, and in view of his appearing and his kingdom, I give you this charge: Preach the word; be prepared in season and out of season; correct, rebuke and encourage—with great patience and careful instruction. For the time will come when people will not put up with sound doctrine. Instead, to suit their own desires, they will gather around them a great number of teachers to say what their itching ears want to hear. They will turn their ears away from the truth and turn aside to myths. But you, keep your head in all situations, endure hardship, do the work of an evangelist, discharge all the duties of your ministry. (2 Timothy 4:1–5)

Messages from James

Jesus had several brothers (or half-brothers) who became missionaries on behalf of their Lord. One of them, James, wrote an intensely practical epistle. Here is a selection of his teaching:

> Religion that God our Father accepts as pure and faultless is this: to look after orphans and widows in their distress and to keep oneself from being polluted by the world.
>
> My brothers and sisters, believers in our glorious Lord Jesus Christ must not show favoritism. Suppose a man comes into your meeting wearing a gold ring and fine clothes, and a poor man in filthy old clothes also comes

in. If you show special attention to the man wearing fine clothes and say, "Here's a good seat for you," but say to the poor man, "You stand there" or "Sit on the floor by my feet," have you not discriminated among yourselves and become judges with evil thoughts?

Listen, my dear brothers and sisters: Has not God chosen those who are poor in the eyes of the world to be rich in faith and to inherit the kingdom he promised those who love him? But you have dishonored the poor. Is it not the rich who are exploiting you? Are they not the ones who are dragging you into court? Are they not the ones who are blaspheming the noble name of him to whom you belong?

If you really keep the royal law found in Scripture, "Love your neighbor as yourself," you are doing right. But if you show favoritism, you sin and are convicted by the law as lawbreakers. (James 1:27 – 2:9)

When we put bits into the mouths of horses to make them obey us, we can turn the whole animal. Or take ships as an example. Although they are so large and are driven by strong winds, they are steered by a very small rudder wherever the pilot wants to go. Likewise, the tongue is a small part of the body, but it makes great boasts. Consider what a great forest is set on fire by a small spark. The tongue also is a fire, a world of evil among the parts of the body. It corrupts the whole body, sets the whole course of one's life on fire, and is itself set on fire by hell.

All kinds of animals, birds, reptiles and sea creatures are being tamed and have been tamed by mankind, but no human being can tame the tongue. It is a restless evil, full of deadly poison.

With the tongue we praise our Lord and Father, and

with it we curse human beings, who have been made in God's likeness. Out of the same mouth come praise and cursing. My brothers and sisters, this should not be. Can both fresh water and salt water flow from the same spring? My brothers and sisters, can a fig tree bear olives, or a grapevine bear figs? Neither can a salt spring produce fresh water. (James 3:3 – 12)

A Message from Peter

The apostle Peter addresses Christian communities throughout what we now call Turkey, who were beginning to experience imperial pressure. He calls on them stand up for Christ and to continue to show love:

Finally, all of you, be like-minded, be sympathetic, love one another, be compassionate and humble. Do not repay evil with evil or insult with insult. On the contrary, repay evil with blessing, because to this you were called so that you may inherit a blessing. For [here Peter quotes Psalm 33 from the Old Testament],

"Whoever would love life
and see good days
must keep their tongue from evil
and their lips from deceitful speech.
They must turn from evil and do good;
they must seek peace and pursue it.
For the eyes of the Lord are on the righteous
and his ears are attentive to their prayer,
but the face of the Lord is against those who do evil."

Who is going to harm you if you are eager to do good? But even if you should suffer for what is right, you are blessed. "Do not fear their threats; do not be frightened." But in your hearts revere Christ as Lord. Always be prepared to give an answer to everyone who asks you to give the reason for the hope that you have. But do this with gentleness and respect, keeping a clear conscience, so that those who speak maliciously against your good behavior in Christ may be ashamed of their slander. For it is better, if it is God's will, to suffer for doing good than for doing evil. (1 Peter 3:8–17)

A Message from John

The apostle John reflects on the tangibility of Jesus (whom he had heard and touched personally), on the wonder of forgiveness of sins, and on the duty to love others:

> That which was from the beginning, which we have heard, which we have seen with our eyes, which we have looked at and our hands have touched — this we proclaim concerning the Word of life. The life appeared; we have seen it and testify to it, and we proclaim to you the eternal life, which was with the Father and has appeared to us. We proclaim to you what we have seen and heard, so that you also may have fellowship with us. And our fellowship is with the Father and with his Son, Jesus Christ. We write this to make our joy complete.

> This is the message we have heard from him and declare to you: God is light; in him there is no darkness at all. If we claim to have fellowship with him and yet walk in the darkness, we lie and do not live out the truth. But if we walk in the light, as he is in the light, we have fellowship with one another, and the blood of Jesus, his Son, purifies us from all sin.

If we claim to be without sin, we deceive ourselves and the truth is not in us. If we confess our sins, he is faithful and just and will forgive us our sins and purify us from all unrighteousness. If we claim we have not sinned, we make him out to be a liar and his word is not in us.

My dear children, I write this to you so that you will not sin. But if anybody does sin, we have an advocate with the Father — Jesus Christ, the Righteous One. He is the atoning sacrifice for our sins, and not only for ours but also for the sins of the whole world.

We know that we have come to know him if we keep his commands. Whoever says, "I know him," but does not do what he commands is a liar, and the truth is not in that person. But if anyone obeys his word, love for God is truly made complete in them. This is how we know we are in him: Whoever claims to live in him must live as Jesus did.

Dear friends, I am not writing you a new command but an old one, which you have had since the beginning. This old command is the message you have heard. Yet I am writing you a new command; its truth is seen in him and in you, because the darkness is passing and the true light is already shining.

Anyone who claims to be in the light but hates a brother or sister is still in the darkness. Anyone who loves their brother and sister lives in the light, and there is nothing in them to make them stumble. But anyone who hates a brother or sister is in the darkness and walks around in the darkness. They do not know where they are going, because the darkness has blinded them. (1 John 1:1 – 2:11)

The letters of the New Testament — whether those by Paul, James, Peter, or John — were written to instruct

Christians about how to believe and behave as they serve this world and wait for the kingdom of God to appear. The premise of all the letters is that Jesus' death and resurrection guarantee our place in the future kingdom, and his life and teaching provide a glimpse of what it means to live for that kingdom in this period of amnesty, this era of mission to the nations. The epistles do not answer every dilemma a modern person might ask about following Christ in this day and age, but they certainly provide great inspiration and a compelling framework for living out what it means to be a person of faith in every area of life.

10

HOW EVERYTHING IS GOOD AGAIN: THE RE-CREATION STORY

HE WILL WIPE EVERY TEAR FROM THEIR EYES. THERE WILL BE NO MORE
DEATH OR MOURNING OR CRYING OR PAIN, FOR THE OLD ORDER OF
THINGS HAS PASSED AWAY.

(REVELATION 21:4)

ULTIMATE QUESTIONS

I pointed out at the start of this book that the Bible is the
most popular publication of all time — another thirty million or more have sold since I started writing this book
twelve months ago — and I explained this extraordinary
fact by claiming that the Bible tells a story we recognize as
true. Its account of the human dilemma and the shape of its
answer ring true at a profound level, at least for millions of
people throughout history and today. Reading the Bible can
be like walking into a new café desperate for your coffee fix

and finding the barista standing there holding your favorite double shot latte with one sugar. This book knows us.

It begins from the opening scenes. Adam was made for relationship with God, connection with others, and enjoyment of the garden. The spiritual, social, and physical dimensions of existence are as they should be, as we long for them to be. "Curiosity about our beginning," writes theologian Henri Blocher, "continues to haunt the human race. It will not call off the Quest for its origins" (Henri Blocher, *In the Beginning: The Opening Chapters of Genesis* [InterVarsity Press, 1984], 15). While a *scientific* understanding of origins is exciting and meaningful—and something of a luxury in the "blip" of the last 150 years—the real human pursuit has been to understand why we are here, what purpose it serves, what direction we're heading in, and what significance it all has. Science, for all its wonders, is incapable of approaching such questions, and we dishonor science by imagining it is otherwise.

We also dishonor ourselves by imagining science's questions and answers are the only important ones. This is an important point to ponder in our contemporary context, because there are some strands of thought (and talk) that suggest the only significant questions are the ones science can investigate. This cannot be the case. As philosopher Alvin Plantinga humorously suggests, this would be like a drunk man insisting on looking for his lost car keys only under a lamppost because that's where the light is shining. "In fact it would go the drunk one better," Plantinga quips; "it would be to insist that because the keys would be hard to find in the dark, they must be under the light" (Alvin

Plantinga, *Warranted Christian Belief* [Oxford University Press, 2000], 406). Science sheds its wonderful light on the operations of the natural world, but it is seriously restrictive to imagine that no keys to important questions can be found outside its gleam.

Genesis tells us about *origins*, in the theological and philosophical sense of why we're here and what it means. But, oddly, it also tells us where we are headed. The picture painted in the garden of social, spiritual, and environmental harmony is as much about the future as it is about the past. It concerns creation's goal, not just its starting point.

I like to think of the opening chapters of the Bible as a model of the healthy heart, which a cardiologist might show patients in order to explain the *problem* with their heart and the *goal* of the treatment. Genesis 1 and 2 provide the model of health in the spiritual, social, and physical dimensions. That being so, Genesis 3, the fall, offers a kind of "diagnosis." Adam defies God and so begins the undoing of our relationship with the Creator, with each other, and with the physical creation itself. This is the human condition, estranged from our source, estranged from one another, and frustrated in our environment. The diagnosis rings true, and only the dewy-eyed utopian could imagine we're on a trajectory of recovery all on our own.

The rest of the Bible, this vast story, concerns God's remedy—in biblical speak, "redemption." Redemption in the Bible is not just a *spiritual* rescue. It involves all three dimensions we have been exploring throughout this book. God intends to redeem our relationship with him, our connections with one another, and our enjoyment of creation itself.

As we move through the Old Testament, Israel's story — from Abraham to David and beyond — is a preview or a sign of this redemptive plan. Built into the fabric of the Old Testament itself is the idea that Israel is a microcosm of what God will do for the whole world. The promise to Abraham in Genesis 12:1 – 3 concerned blessing from God, a new community, and fruitful land. Through Abraham these blessings would somehow come to "all peoples on earth." This is the threefold promise of the Bible.

The New Testament reiterates the promise and declares that it all comes to realization in Jesus, the descendant of Abraham, from the line of King David. In a majestic statement in his letter to the Colossians (Colossae is in southwest Turkey) about thirty years after Jesus (early AD 60s), the apostle Paul speaks of the "cosmic" effects of the work of the Messiah:

> He is before all things, and in him all things hold together. And he is the head of the body, the church; he is the beginning and the firstborn from among the dead, so that in everything he might have the supremacy. For God was pleased to have all his fullness dwell in him, and through him to reconcile to himself all things, whether things on earth or things in heaven, by making peace through his blood, shed on the cross. (Colossians 1:17 – 20)

The Bible's redemptive plan is not just about putting souls into heaven. God wants to redeem *all* things, whether things on earth or things in heaven — which doesn't leave much else!

NEW CREATION

In short, the biblical narrative moves from *creation* to *new creation*, which is why the last two chapters of the Bible (Revelation 21–22) are replete with allusions to the first two chapters of the Bible (Genesis 1–2). The book of Revelation is mostly written in a style known as "apocalyptic," a well-known literary type among Jews of the ancient world. Using figurative language and images, apocalyptic literature was able to encourage people—frequently oppressed people—that despite circumstances, God is in control and will keep his promises to the faithful. Toward the end of the book, the author describes a vision in which he sees "a new heaven and a new earth," clearly intended to echo the opening line of the Bible ("In the beginning God created the heavens and the earth," Genesis 1:1):

> Then I saw "a new heaven and a new earth," for the first heaven and the first earth had passed away, and there was no longer any sea. I saw the Holy City, the new Jerusalem, coming down out of heaven from God, prepared as a bride beautifully dressed for her husband. And I heard a loud voice from the throne saying, "Look! God's dwelling place is now among the people, and he will dwell with them. They will be his people, and God himself will be with them and be their God. 'He will wipe every tear from their eyes. There will be no more death' or mourning or crying or pain, for the old order of things has passed away."
>
> He who was seated on the throne said, "I am making everything new!" (Revelation 21:1–5)

The idea of God "dwelling with people" recalls the

picture of Genesis 2, where the Lord God dwelt in the garden with Adam and Eve. We could continue on with this apocalyptic vision through Revelation 22 — the final chapter of the Bible — where we find a garden, rivers, and the tree of life. All of these are features of Eden in the opening chapters of the Bible. Despite the evocative imagery used throughout the vision, the general point is plain: God intends to recover Eden for all. From "creation" to "new creation" — this is the story line of the Bible.

Jesus himself put this majestic, cosmic story line in a single word, one that is difficult to translate adequately into English. In Matthew 19:28 he says, "Truly I tell you, at *the renewal of all things*, when the Son of Man sits on his glorious throne, you who have followed me will also sit on twelve thrones, judging the twelve tribes of Israel." The words "renewal of all things" translate a single Greek term, *palingenesia*, which is a combination of the words *palin* or "again" and *genesia* or "production/genesis." I like to think of it as "genesis again," for this is exactly what the Bible, from Genesis to Revelation, envisages: God will renew and redeem not just souls but the whole creation.

Centuries before Jesus, this is exactly what the prophet Isaiah promised:

> See, I will create
> new heavens and a new earth.
> The former things will not be remembered,
> nor will they come to mind.
> But be glad and rejoice forever
> in what I will create,
> for I will create Jerusalem to be a delight,

and its people a joy.
I will rejoice over Jerusalem
    and take delight in my people,
the sound of weeping and of crying
    will be heard in it no more.
Never again will there be in it
    an infant who lives but a few days,
    or an old man who does not live out his years;
the one who dies at a hundred
    will be thought a mere child....
They will build houses and dwell in them.
    They will plant vineyards and eat their fruit.
No longer will they build houses and others live in
      them,
    or plant and others eat ...
for they will be a people blessed by the Lord,
    they and their descendants with them.
Before they call I will answer;
    while they are still speaking I will hear.
The wolf and the lamb will feed together
    and the lion will eat straw like the ox,
    and dust will be the serpent's food.
They will neither harm nor destroy
    on all my holy mountain,
           says the Lord." (Isaiah 65:17 – 25)

Obviously, there are figures of speech throughout Isaiah 65. It is a poem in the original Hebrew. The expression "the one who dies at a hundred will be thought a mere child" does not mean people will die in God's future kingdom. It is literary understatement — litotes, for the technically minded, the opposite of the hyperbole.

What about "the wolf and the lamb will feed together"? No doubt this is poetic, but poetic of what? It may be a straight metaphor for warring nations at peace. Then again, it may be a concrete symbol of the renewal of the animal kingdom, for in Genesis 1–2, from which Isaiah's vision draws so much, you also have Adam in harmony with the animal kingdom. "Do dogs go to heaven?" may not be as silly a theological question as it sometimes sounds.

Whatever the literary figures of Isaiah's poetic description of the kingdom come, they are all figures of speech designed to underline not the removal of creation but its redemption. Just as Genesis 1 and 2 use symbolism and metaphor to say things about a real creation, so Isaiah uses poetry, hyperbole, and litotes to speak of the redemption of creation. The Bible's idea of the "kingdom come" concerns the restoration of the spiritual, social, and physical dimensions of existence, or what Jesus called the *palingenesia* (genesis again), the renewal of all things.

The reason I am stressing this—even if none of it is news to some readers—is that the contemporary picture of the afterlife tends to come from a weird combination of Greek philosophy, eastern religion, and Hollywood. The Greek philosopher Plato promoted the view that physical existence was a diminished reflection of the true *mental* reality toward which all the universe is heading. The Greek tradition downplayed the importance of the body, of physicality, both in the present life and the afterlife. Paradoxically, this led either to *asceticism*, the harsh treatment of the body, or to *hedonism*, the use of the body for any pleasure on the grounds that bodily existence does not ultimately matter.

Eastern religion teaches much the same thing. Salvation in Hinduism is called *moksha*. It is the liberation of the soul *from* bodily existence, so that the worthy one might merge with the spirit behind the universe, Brahman, like a spark returning to its flame or a drop of water being engulfed by the ocean. Nirvana in Buddhism shares the same basic premise, for the Buddha described the ultimate goal as a cessation of all matter and sensation.

Somehow Hollywood got hold of all of these ideas — together with a few biblical ones thrown in — and routinely portrays the afterlife as an ethereal, ghostly, nonbodily reality with some harp music playing in the background.

All of this is far from the consistent picture of the future found in the Bible, whether Isaiah's new heaven and earth, Jesus' *palingenesia*, or Revelation's new creation. A statement of the apostle Paul from the middle of the first century drives the point home in highly theological language:

> For the creation waits in eager expectation for the children of God to be revealed. For the creation was subjected to frustration, not by its own choice, but by the will of the one who subjected it, in hope that the creation itself will be liberated from its bondage to decay and brought into the freedom and glory of the children of God. (Romans 8:19–21)

The biblical hope is not liberation *from* creation, but the liberation *of* creation. The creation is waiting for its own deliverance, Paul says. It will be brought into the glorious freedom of the children of God, he adds. That may sound strange, but the apostle just means that the creation will undergo a kind of "resurrection," just as God's people will experience resurrection. Eternal life is not disembodied life; it is bodily life guaranteed by Christ's own resurrection. The doctrine of the resurrection of the body ties in with the equally important doctrine of the renewal of creation. In fact, where else can you live out a resurrection body but in a new creation?

This is why the Nicene Creed, the famous creed affirmed by all Roman Catholics and Protestants to this day, climaxes in this statement: "We look forward to the resurrection of the dead and the life of the world to come." This is not a statement about Christ's resurrection (mentioned earlier in this creed) but *ours*. Christianity from the beginning insisted that God intends to restore everything. In Christ, all the hopes of humanity—for connection with God, reconciliation with each other, and the renewal of creation itself—are realized.

BOOK NOTES

One excellent book on the physical nature of the Bible's teaching about "heaven" or, more properly, "the kingdom of God," is N. T. Wright's *Surprised by Hope: Rethinking Heaven, the Resurrection, and the Mission of the Church* (HarperOne, 2008). One (slight) criticism I have of this book is the impression it occasionally gives that its contents are a "revision" or "rethinking" of traditional biblical views of the future kingdom, when they are in fact just the standard beliefs of Christians from earliest times—even if sometimes overlooked by contemporary believers.

NEW CREATION AND THE WEAKNESS OF DEATH

Christians live in light of the fact that this world is not all there is, and they try to live in a balance between future hope and present activity. Christians should not be so heavenly minded that they are of no earthly use, but neither should they be so earthly minded that they forget the "kingdom come." True Christianity holds both in beautiful tension. But how so?

Christians believe the lifespan of each of us is not the full running length; it is a kind of preview. They believe that the human injustice that infects everything in the world will find an ultimate answer in God's justice. They believe that the groanings of an afflicted creation will be answered when God recreates the world in glory.

These beliefs change what a person thinks, the way they live, who they are. Death, says the Christian, is not the end. John Donne articulated the Christian view of death in one of his poems:

> Death be not proud, though some have called thee
> Mighty and dreadful, for thou art not so;
> For many whom thou think'st thou dost overthrow
> Die not, poor Death, nor yet canst thou kill me ...
> One short sleep past, we wake eternally
> And death shall be no more; Death, thou shalt die.
> (John Donne, *Death Be Not Proud*, 1610)

Donne could pen such words and Christians can echo his sentiment because they believe in resurrection, Christ's and ours, and that of the whole creation.

Recently, I was regularly visiting a dying friend, James,

in Greenwich Hospital, Sydney. I noticed a change in him one week. His body was wasting away, but he started to talk more and more openly about his hope for the coming kingdom, about the hope of the resurrection. We had wonderful chats about what God would do in the future, what God has promised. This man, who had been a judge in Sydney for twenty years, came to believe firmly in God's coming kingdom. I had the great privilege of leading his funeral and telling all of his judicial friends, "James believed this is not all there is. James believed in the coming kingdom." My words followed eulogy upon eulogy describing him as a "man of impeccably good legal judgment." I suggested that his greatest judgment concerned the trustworthiness of the Bible's testimony about the future.

Three days before he died, I visited James. He was in a morphine stupor and I sheepishly asked, "James, it's John. Would you like me to pray with you?" He opened his eyes and shot his hand up through the sheets, grabbed hold of my hand, and for about thirty seconds was more conscious than he'd been in days. I prayed for a miracle, and I thanked God for the greater miracle of the resurrection of the body and the renewal of all things. By the time I said "Amen" he was back into his morphine haze. But, as I told his colleagues at the funeral, James has ample opportunity to say "Amen" now.

NEW CREATION AND THE POWER TO LIVE

The doctrine of the renewal of creation is not simply for the dying. When the Bible speaks about the future kingdom, it often talks about what it means for us to *live* in light of what is to come. Future hope impinges on our ethics—but not the way people often imagine.

People sometimes talk as though the correlation between heaven and ethics is similar to the one between payday and the working week. "You better be good," they say, "or God might not let you in to heaven." Alan Dershowitz, a law professor at Harvard University, critiques Christianity on precisely this point, in the last entry in his *Letters to a Young Lawyer* (Basic Books, 2001, 193–200). He argues that believers do good with *impure* motives, since they're trying to gain eternal rewards or avoid eternal punishments. This is ultimately selfish. Only the atheist, he says, who believes in neither eternal reward nor punishment, is able to be truly moral, for when an atheist does a good act, he or she does so "simply because it was deemed by the actor to be good."

I like the cheeky, subversive style of the writing. It would be a good argument *if that's what Christianity actually taught*! But the Christian life is not motivated by reward and punishment. It is inspired by gratitude for the favor God has already bestowed. This is basic to the biblical narrative, as we have seen over and over again. From Abraham to Jesus, God offers his grace first and then expects our obedience to follow. Christians give to the poor, not because they're trying to pay their way to heaven but out of thankfulness for all that God has given. They feel compassion for detained refugees not for fear of their own detention in hell but in appreciation of the fact that the Creator loves all people.

Even when the Bible does draw a link between God's future kingdom and our present behavior, it does so with a logic different from that mocked by Professor Dershowitz.

The relationship between the coming kingdom and current ethics has nothing to do with trying to win a place in heaven. It is about trying to live now by the realities that will prevail for eternity. The future kingdom will be one of righteousness, love, peace, and grace, so Christians try to live righteous, loving, peaceful, gracious lives while they wait for the kingdom to be realized. Christians believe that a new dawn is breaking and so they try to live like the glorious new day is already here. This is exactly how Paul puts it in a passage that is simultaneously about the future kingdom and current behavior:

> Love does no harm to a neighbor. Therefore love is the fulfillment of the law.
>
> And do this [i.e., practice this love], understanding the present time: The hour has already come for you to wake up from your slumber, because our salvation is nearer now than when we first believed. The night is nearly over; the day is almost here. So let us put aside the deeds of darkness and put on the armor of light. Let us behave decently, as in the daytime, not in carousing and drunkenness, not in sexual immorality and debauchery, not in dissension and jealousy. Rather, clothe yourselves with the Lord Jesus Christ, and do not think about how to gratify the desires of the flesh. (Romans 13:10 – 14)

It is because a kingdom of love is coming and will prevail over everything that Christians get busy now embodying that love in all that they do (at least, in theory). A similar thing was taught by the apostle Peter about the same time Paul wrote the above: "we are looking forward to a new heaven and a new earth, where righteousness dwells.

So then, dear friends, since you are looking forward to this, make every effort to be found spotless, blameless and at peace with him" (2 Peter 3:13–14). Peter's logic isn't that we need to live good lives so that we can get into the "new heaven and [the] earth, where righteousness dwells"; he says we live righteous lives *because we are looking forward* to this kind of kingdom. No Christian earns their way into heaven; rather, *heaven works its way into the Christian.*

BUT IS IT ALL WISHFUL THINKING?

In *The Weight of Glory* C. S. Lewis describes humanity as having a sort of longing for a far-off country, which some people dismiss as nostalgia or romanticism but which he thinks comes because we were made for heaven. "Almost all our education has been directed to silencing this shy, persistent inner voice," he says; "almost all our modern philosophies have been devised to convince us that the good of man is to be found on this earth." But Lewis says we are never satisfied with earth as it is, with all its discord and sadness. Christians look beyond the pain, for "all the leaves of the New Testament are rustling with the rumor that it will not always be so" (C. S. Lewis, *The Weight of Glory* [HarperOne, 2001], 31).

Just about every culture we know anything significant about has made three questions a core part of its philosophical curiosity. How do we connect with our Source? How do we get along with one another? How will the pain of material existence be resolved? It seems that these are the universal questions, and I have been trying to show throughout this book that the Bible offers a deliberate and comprehensive set of answers. From Genesis 1–2 to Revelation 21–22—the bookends of the Bible—Christian Scripture says the Creator has disclosed how we can be reconciled to him, how human communities can flourish, and how creation itself will be restored. That is the story of the Bible.

But we all know there is a cynical interpretation of all this. "Of course, humans have always had such longings. This is why they invent religion and project their desires onto that fantasy." Religion, the argument goes, is just wish-fulfillment, humans inventing stories to satisfy their existential thirst.

The idea of religion as a wish-fulfillment is repeated so often in our culture that some just accept it as a grand truism. In the modern world it came into our culture through two men, both Germans. Ludwig Feuerbach in the 1840s wrote a book called *Natural Religion*, in which he argued that religion, specifically Christianity, is a wish-fulfillment. Sigmund Freud picked up this idea and psychologized it. He said that our deep psychological desires are transposed into our religious wish-fulfillment. We long for a "father" or a "mother" in the sky and so project the longings onto a "god." At the time, people cheekily asked the obvious question. What about Freud's and Feuerbach's atheism? Couldn't that just as easily be a wish-fulfillment—a desire for there to be no "god," no lord above us, and this manifests itself in the conviction that God is merely a wish-fulfillment?

The fact that humans have longings for God, the afterlife, and ethics tells you nothing about whether these things are real. The fact that humanity has longings that are satisfied by the teaching of the Bible is no more an argument against the Bible than physical thirst can be thought of as an argument against the reality of water. Observing that I have a thirst does not explain away H_2O.

BOOK NOTES

Perhaps the best book (still) drawing the lines between our inner longings and the basics of Christianity is C. S. Lewis, *Mere Christianity* (HarperCollins, 1997). My wife and I continue to draw insight and inspiration from this book—I often remark how "Clive" is her other husband! It was originally written during wartime Britain but preempts questions and complaints that are surprisingly current.

Perhaps the skeptics are right: the way the Bible answers humanity's longings is to be explained away by the fact that people with just those desires *created* the Bible in the first place (even with all its unified complexity). Then again, perhaps this "match" between human longings and the Bible's message arises because the one who made us for himself stands behind the Bible, as water for our thirst. In his *Confessions,* one of the most influential books of Western history, Saint Augustine wrote poignantly of human restlessness and the "rest" that is only found in the Creator:

> Man is one of your creatures, Lord, and his instinct is to praise you. The thought of you stirs him so deeply that he cannot be content unless he praises you, because you made us for yourself and our hearts find no peace until they rest in you. (Saint Augustine, *Confessions* [Penguin Classics, 1961], 21).

Our hearts are restless until they find their rest in God. Augustine's argument, 1,400 years before Feuerbach, was that Christianity is most certainly a wish-fulfillment—it is a *true* wish-fulfillment.

If this were a different kind of book, I would explain why I think it is reasonable to trust the Bible as a *true* wish-fulfillment, water for humanity's thirst. Perhaps I would begin with the miracle that is the Bible itself. The fact that so many different authors, over such a vast period of time, in totally different cultures, through a variety of literary genres, have come up with such a coherent, comprehensive answer to humanity's longings is, for me, beyond uncanny. Then I might turn to the history of Jesus and point out, as I have done in other books mentioned earlier, that we have pretty much the kind of evidence you would expect if the Gospels' account of Christ is true, and much more evidence pointing in that direction than you would expect if the Gospels were false.

But this is not that kind of book. I said at the outset, this is not intended as a work of "apologetics"—the art of trying to prove the truth of the Bible. It is an attempt to explain to curious doubters what it might mean if the Bible turned out to be true. Here at the end, then, I am content simply to leave readers with the idea, embraced by countless millions of men, women, and children throughout history, that in Jesus Christ all of our longings *for God*, *for each other*, and *for the redemption of creation* are satisfied. He is water for my thirst.

And so it seems fitting that in the final lines of the book of Revelation, the final lines of the Bible itself, we are all invited for a drink—and with these words I end:

> Let the one who is thirsty, come; and let the one who wishes take the free gift of the water of life. (Revelation 22:17)

Christ Files

How Historians Know What They Know about Jesus

John Dickson

The Christ Files, a four-session small group Bible study, scholar John Dickson examines the Christian faith through a historical look at the Christian faith and life of Jesus from both Scriptural and other non-Bible documentation.

Unique among the world's religions, the central claims of Christianity concern not just timeless spiritual truths, but tangible historical events as well. Historian John Dickson examines Christianity's claims in the light of history, opening you and your group to a wealth of ancient sources and explaining how mainstream scholars—whether or not they claim Christian Faith personally—reach their conclusions about history's most influential figure, Jesus of Nazareth.

The Christ Files will help you and your small group expand your understanding of early Christianity and the life of Jesus.

This 110-page participant guide includes seven chapters of reading and background contextual information, along with questions for four impactful small group sessions. It is meant for use in conjunction with the four-session *The Christ Files DVD* (sold separately).

Available in stores and online!

Life of Jesus
Who He Is and Why He Matters

John Dickson

What really happened back in the first century, in Jerusalem and around the Sea of Galilee, that changed the shape of world history? Who is this figure that emerges from history to have a profound impact on culture, ethics, politics, and philosophy? Join historian John Dickson on this journey through the life of Jesus.

This book, which features a self-contained discussion guide for use with *Life of Jesus* DVD (available separately), will help you and your friends dig deeper into what is known about Jesus' life and why it matters.

"John Dickson has done a marvelous job of presenting the story of Jesus, and the full meaning of that story, in a way that is both deeply faithful to the biblical sources and refreshingly relevant to tomorrow's world and church. I strongly recommend this study to anyone who wants to re-examine the deep historical roots of Christian faith and to find them as life-giving as they ever were."—Tom Wright

Available in stores and online!

ZONDERVAN®
.com

Best Kept Secret of Christian Mission

Promoting the Gospel with More Than Our Lips

John Dickson

Forewords by ALISTER MCGRATH & RAVI ZACHARIAS

JOHN DICKSON

The Best Kept Secret of
Christian Mission

Promoting the Gospel with More Than Our Lips

This book comes out of years of reflection, failures, and some successes in the task of reaching out to others with the gospel.

In this practical guide to the biblical art of sharing your faith, John Dickson offers refreshing insight into the ways that all Christians can and should be involved in spreading the good news of Jesus. While not all Christians are called and gifted to become evangelists, we are all called to promote the gospel through a wide range of activities—prayer, financial partnership, good deeds, godly lives, public worship, daily conversation, etc.—with and without our lips.

As readers engage with this book, grapple with its arguments and hear the stories of people coming to faith, they will be inspired to see the whole of life as significant for bringing the gospel to the world, and they will be liberated out of guilt and self-consciousness in evangelism into becoming perfectly natural promoters of Jesus Christ.

Available in stores and online!

Humilitas

A Lost Key to Life, Love, and Leadership

John Dickson

Humility, or holding power loosely for the sake of others, is sorely lacking in today's world. Without it, many people fail to develop their true leadership potential and miss out on genuine fulfillment in their lives and their relationships. *Humilitas: A Lost Key to Life, Love, and Leadership* shows how the virtue of humility can turn your strengths into true greatness in all areas of life. Through the lessons of history, business, and the social sciences, author John Dickson shows that humility is not low self-esteem, groveling, or losing our distinct gifts. Instead, humility both recognizes our inherent worth and seeks to use whatever power we have at our disposal on behalf of others. Some of the world's most inspiring and influential players have been people of immense humility. The more we learn about humility, the more we understand how essential it is to a satisfying career and personal life. By embracing this virtue, we will transform for good the unique contributions we each make to the world.

Available in stores and online!

Fresh Perspectives on Women in Ministry

Hearing Her Voice, Revised Edition

A Case for Women Giving Sermons

John Dickson

A fresh approach to the hot-button topic of women in ministry

Based on his study of a key word for "teaching" in the New Testament—an activity often thought to be prohibited to women—and on various other kinds of public speaking in which women in Scripture clearly participated, scholar John Dickson builds a case for women preachers.

This expanded edition of *Hearing Her Voice*, published originally as a short ebook, presents an entirely new and convincing biblical argument. Focused and purposefully limited in its conclusions, Dickson's case has the potential to change minds and merits careful consideration by complementarians and egalitarians alike.

This book will be useful for pastors, Bible teachers, college and seminary students, professors, and lay leaders who wrestle with the topic of women's roles in ministry, and it will appeal to many with its fresh approach to this hot-button topic.

Available in stores and online!

ZONDERVAN®
.com